Items should be returned on or before the last date shown below. Items not already requested by other borrowers may be renewed in person, in writing or by telephone. To renew, please quote the number on the barcode label. To renew online a PIN is required. This can be requested at your local library.
Renew online @ **www.dublincitypubliclibraries.ie**
Fines charged for overdue items will include postage incurred in recovery. Damage to or loss of items will be charged to the borrower.

**Leabharlanna Poiblí Chathair Bhaile Átha Cliath
Dublin City Public Libraries**

Dublin City
Baile Átha Cliath

Marino Branch
Brainse Marglann Mhuiríne
Tel: 8336297

Date Due	Date Due	Date Due
21. NOV 12		
30. MAY 14;		

D1440319

This edition published 2012
by Poolbeg Press Ltd
123 Grange Hill, Baldoyle
Dublin 13, Ireland
E-mail: poolbeg@poolbeg.com
www.poolbeg.com

© Bill Kelly 1983, 1987, 2012

Copyright for typesetting, layout, design, ebook
© Poolbeg Press Ltd

The moral right of the author has been asserted.

1 3 5 7 9 10 8 6 4 2

A catalogue record for this book is available from the British Library.

ISBN 978-1-84223-566-9

Cover design and typesetting by Poolbeg Press

Printed and bound by
CPI Group (UK) Ltd, Croydon, CR0 4YY

www.poolbeg.com

About the author

Bill Kelly was born in Dublin in 1922 as the embryonic and scarred Free State was taking its first tentative steps as a member of the international community. The War of Independence and the Civil War had wreaked havoc on many parts of the capital city and the country generally, but as a child growing up in the twenties and the thirties, Bill's fertile imagination was fuelled by his love of reading, and the cinema.

Football was another passion, and he joined Home Farm FC in 1934. He was educated by nuns in Gardiner Street and later by the Christian Brothers. Shortly before the Second World War he got his first job in the former Department of Posts and Telegraphs, or "the Post Office" as it was colloquially known. His real love was writing, and he liked it even better when the got paid for it! His introduction to journalism came in the newsroom of Radio Éireann in 1946. For many years he led a double life, working by day in the Telecommunications Branch of the P & T, and working in journalism by night.

In 1953 he began writing a soccer column for the *Sunday Press* as "Big Bill" and the column ran for 30 years. At its peak in 1973 the *Sunday Press* was selling 432,000 copies each week.

Bill was a prolific and committed writer. He contributed features for leading newspapers and magazines in Ireland and Britain, and was a spare-time editor, ghost-writer and book reviewer. A student of the War of Independence, he interviewed many veterans of that conflict and wrote on the subject for Anvil Books and *The Kerryman*.

Through it all, he was happiest when rambling around Dublin, meeting cronies and friends, and putting the world to rights. He passed away in August 1996.

Contents

Chapter 1

Me Darlin' Dublin's Dead and Gone

You always knew it was Friday. Every Friday a little man in a dustcoat and cloth cap stood outside Bill Bushe's pub at the cornet of Gardiner Street and rendered "Roses of Picardy" on a comet – the musical type, not the ice-cream. He carried a collecting box which pleaded, "Help an ex-Serviceman", but the help he could expect from the denizens of Dorset Street in the early twenties was meagre, because the people who might have contributed – the other British ex-servicemen – had as much as he had, which was sweet nothing. And the others, the ones who hadn't gone away to fight for the King and Empire, wouldn't have helped him even if they had it. For some of them had fought against the King and his Empire in the vicious bitter bloody Tan War, and they wouldn't help. And others, those who had fought neither for nor against His Britannic Majesty wouldn't have helped him on principle (the principle of self-interest, which is what Irish people generally mean when they talk of "principle"), that they had managed to walk the tightrope of neutrality and they weren't about to rock the boat at this stage. You always knew it was Friday, too, because dinner on Fridays was a saucer of rice, and for dessert, a ha'penny chocolate biscuit: a Lucullan feast for a six-year-old slum dweller.

1

You always knew it was Friday in the tenements, because every Friday each woman scrubbed her own landing and flight of stairs and the whole place reeked of Jeyeses Fluid.

Dorset Street was as far in spirit as it was geographically from that lovely county in England from which it took its name. It was a long wide street, stretching from Granby Row to Binn's Bridge across the canal, which divided semi-suburban Drumcondra from the slums. Apart from the shops, which were mainly on the right-hand side of the street as you headed north towards Swords and, at the outer limits of the imagination, Belfast, the Georgian houses of Dorset Street, which had once accommodated the petit bourgeoisie and traders, had long since given up the pretence of being the relics of oul' dacency, and sadly and resignedly accepted their tenement status.

They've all been levelled now, but the people who lived in them, those who survived the consumption long enough to escape, will never forget them. For you can never forget the feel of a tenement. More, you never quite get the smell of a tenement out of your nostrils. It's a smell of damp and decay, of deep-rooted dust and poverty, of urine and red raddle, and above all of hopelessness. Hopelessness, just fringing on despair, but not quite despair, because every room in the house, each one occupied by a different family, kept the "colzoil" lamp with the red shade burning in front of the ubiquitous picture or statue of the Sacred Heart. And that kept flickering hope just barely alive.

On Fridays, the dealers brought out their wooden barrows from which they sold fresh-Howth-herrins-a-ha'penny-each or Dubalin-Bay-mack'rel-only-a-penny.

The dealers also obliged their tenement neighbours with a loan of a shilling or two, or half-a-crown, to be paid back on

Saturday, from the man's wages, if he was lucky enough to be working, and if it weren't paid on Saturday, "shure it'd be alright, only it's two shillin's or four shillin's or five shillin's next week." A number of them became quite wealthy from the dealing and the money-lending and there's more than one doctor or lawyer or professional man today who doesn't want to trace the family tree back to his grandmother.

The Jewman and the landlord usually came on Friday, and there was some substance to the rumour that these gentry occasionally collected the rent - or the loan repayment in kind, and indeed I remember one coalman – at that time the bellman went on his rounds with the coal in his horse-drawn dray and he measured out the stones of coal at the side of the path – very clearly calling out "coal for cash". It didn't mean anything to me as a snotty kid of six or seven, but in after years, like the eighty-year-old gent sweeping the floor in the county home who flung down the sweeping brush and said, "Blast it, now I know what she meant", it dawned on me.

The dark suspicions and rumours anent the Jewman and landlord erupted in the full glare of public interest when two of the oul' wans, at odds with each other and overburdened with the frustration of existing in what is now described as a deprived environment, would decide to settle their differences in a manly way. But first there was the slanging match in which each wan's ancestry was called into question and then the argumentum descended into ad hominem, or wominem to be more accurate, with banshee-like screeches of "Y'oul hairbater, yeh'll keep away from my childher, y'oul trollop . . . y' hoorsmelt." "Hoorsmelt is it? I was always clean an' dacent, not like some I know when their poor husbands were out at the front fightin'. I never dropped a bastard anyway . . ."

At that stage, the feathers hit the fan, and like two she-elephants disputing a bull in must, they collided in mid-fight, claws grabbing for hair, eyes or clothes, as the neighbours tried to separate them, and the word spread along the street like wildfire – "Ruggy up" – and the crowds poured in from nowhere and we kids scurried from the corners and the backyards and the cellars, to join in the excitement. It was cheap entertainment for the masses, really, and apart from a few tufts of hair missing, neither of the antagonists was injured, though the neighbours would file in their memories for future reference the more outrageous of the accusations cast in the pre-fight ceremonies.

On the Saturday night, however, all was forgiven, at least temporarily and the gladiatoresses could be found in the snug of Bill Bushe's, sipping gills of porter and backbiting.

Five tenements, 83 to 87, housed some fifty families, probably about two hundred people, and it was a close-knit community, though the residents of 83 were a cut above buttermilk because they had a shut hall-door, the outward and visible sign of near-respectability. They could have a shut hall-door because there were only four or five kids in the house altogether, most of the tenants being lonely elderly couples.

In each of the other four houses, there were nine families and hordes of kids, so they couldn't have shut hall-doors. There was one toilet, a noisome whitewashed shed, and one cold water tap in the backyard of each house, and water had to be carried bucket by bucket to each room. Those nearer the top had the tougher job in ferrying water.

Only during the day was the toilet used by the kids, and even the grown-ups trained their bowels to function mainly during the hours of daylight. At night, The Bucket, which stood in The Corner, a recess in each room, served as emergency toilet for the whole family, and only babies were

4

washed in the zinc bath, and that once a week, on Saturday nights, with water heated on the fire, because to heat it on the gas would cost too much.

I can't remember for the first eight years of my life using the backyard toilet at night. Like the other kids in the house, I was afraid. You see, the Mad Oul' Wan lived in the basement, a stone-flagged room under street level, whose window looked out into the area. I suppose in the days when the tenements were occupied by the petit bourgeoisie or traders, this was the kitchen. Up six flights of stairs and six lobbies – the more genteel called them landings – were the front and back top, presumably the skivvies' quarters in the good old days, and, in between, at street level, were the parlour and back parlour. Then the two per front and back, and then the top. I still don't know if it's "per" or "pair" or maybe it was originally a French word sounding something like it.

We were all terrified of the Mad Oul' Wan. She lived alone in the basement, and though she looked the acme of respectability when she went out in the street, dressed in a dark grey serge costume with a black blouse and one of those little round hats Chinamen always wore in the comics, she frequently made forays from the nether regions, lashing out at us kids with a sweeping brush handle as we dashed hell for leather through the hall and up the first two flights of stairs.

We never knew the reason. One day, just as I was going out through the hall, she came in, and I nearly fainted with fright as she stopped in front of me, but she just glared and passed by. When she wasn't terrifying us, she could be heard singing hymns in the fastness of her basement fortress.

The rooms were lit by gas, and when the St Vincent de Paul men were doing their rounds – and God love and bless them, they were sorely needed with their half-dollar food

5

dockets – the gas light was extinguished and the fire doused, and a butt of a candle put flickering on the mantelpiece. Times were so bad that the SVDP men had to look on the ability to put a penny in the gas meter as comparative affluence and most of the families in the block needed their beneficence, though there were the prouder ones who would sooner starve than take their charity. They did.

Looking back, weren't they depriving the SVDP of the chance of performing one of the corporal works of mercy? And if nobody accepted charity, that would be one of the corporal works made redundant.

The older women wore shawls, and were looked down on by the younger married women who felt that only dealers should wear shawls, and it was de rigueur to have a hat and coat for important occasions like going to Mass, or funerals, or Visiting. Visiting meant going at least to the house next door and sitting for a gossip for a couple of hours. You didn't visit the people in the same tenement – usually there was a feud with at least one of them at any given time – and you only "dropped in" on them.

The playwright Sean O'Casey lived around the corner in the North Circular Road, and I've often thought he got his characters from Dorset Street. In the house where he lived there was a Captain Moore of the IRA who once escaped a raid by the British by climbing out the back window and crossing the network of back walls until he reached Sinnott Place. In 87 Dorset Street, there was a Mrs Burgess, whose husband had been fighting "at the Front", as taking part in the first Great War was always called, and who herself had worked in a munitions factory in Arklow during that disturbance. Though her name wasn't Bessie, she was certainly no Shinner.

My impression of O'Casey's Fluther and Joxer was formed

by a living person in No. 85: Diddler, he was called, and he never had a permanent job, though indeed he wasn't unique in that, but always was engaged in some kind of handyman's jobs. He was low-sized, had a brush moustache and always wore a cap and a black muffler, crossed across his chest over a collarless shirt with a bright stud. Apart from F. J. McCormack, the one who came nearest to my mental vision of Fluther was Philip O'Flynn, despite the difference in stature.

There were a couple of Rosies, described, in sotto voce, as "goin' with sailors", and Mollsers were a dime a dozen, though nobody mentioned the dread word "consumption", almost as if it could be contracted by verbal association. It was always a weakness or a decline, but the galloping consumption showed no pity for many with blue eyes and flaxen hair and took them within a matter of weeks.

There was a popular song in the forties that bemoaned Saturday night as the loneliest night of the week. But in Dorset Street in the twenties, Saturday night was the liveliest night in the week, looked forward to as the highlight of the week's entertainment by those who had gallery seats in their tenement windows.

As regularly as clockwork, when at closing time Bushe's pub at the corner of Gardiner Street and McAuley's at the corner of the North Circular Road disgorged their respective clientele through the swing doors, there was one, who, filled with porter and indignation at countless unrighted wrongs, dashed into the middle of the tramlines, flung down his tattered coat, and offered to fight the best man in Dorset Street.

Sometimes his choice would be restricted to a Freestater; at other times it would be an ex-serviceman who took the shillin'; still more rarely, and only if he happened to have been at the front, he'd want a murdherin' bastard of an IRA man who shot dacent men in the back while they were out fightin' at the Front. But mostly it was just a general invitation.

There was always the real danger, if he invited a murdherin' IRA bastard, that there might happen to be one available, and he just might happen to have a gun and the whole complexion of the sport would be altered drastically.

The challenge was usually taken up and most often it would end with a pas de deux of shadow-boxing, coatthrowing on the ground, and verbal threats, after which, honour satisfied, the antagonists and their multifarious seconds would drift homewards. Occasionally, however, the matter came to blows, but the peculiar chivalry of the age didn't allow the use of weapons or boots. If an opponent fell or was knocked down, he prudently stayed prone until the victor was taken away by friends, or until the arrival of two burly DMP men, massive in their darkened night helmets, encumbering capes and fearsome batons in leather sheaths from either Mountjoy or Fitzgibbon Street depending on the location of the ruggy, cleared the street as if by magic.

While the menfolk were in the pub sipping their sixpenny pints, the women had the coddle on the hob, simmering away. Only old women went into the snugs: a respectable woman couldn't, except for a funeral, when she could coyly consent to have a glass of port wine. When the ruggy was over and peace had descended on the street and the men had reached home, the coddle, a recipe peculiar to Dublin – a pound of bacon pieces (6d), a half pound of sausages (3d), a bit of onion and a few potatoes simmered for hours – was eaten. And then it was bed, for there was no television, no wireless, and damn few gramophones, and the gas had to be saved, and the coal had to be stretched, and anyway, it was warmer in bed.

Sunday mornings were different. They were quiet with the hiss and rattle of the occasional tram counterpointed by the tolling of the church bells, and in the clean and uncrowded streets from eight o'clock onwards the people dressed in their Sunday best, though it might well be their weekday worst except that the worn shoes were highly polished, and made their way to Mass. Masses were said every half hour and the last one was at 12 o'clock, except for the one in High Street which took place at 1 o'clock. Twelve Mass was the drunkards' Mass, and many a sorry man suffered the hell of a sore head and the crawsickness at half eleven, rather than admit to being a drunkard. Of course, the well-off people too went to Twelve at which there was all singing of hymns and playing of the organ, but they went into the Sanctuary, which cost threepence, and the lower orders couldn't by any stretch of blasphemy consider them as drunkards, even though they went to Twelve.

My paternal grandfather, Jack, who hailed from County Kildare, was a tall man who sported a walrus moustache and boasted that he had trained Pether Maher. A picture of Pether, stripped to the waist and wearing a sort of tutu, arms bent in front of him with the knuckles turned upwards, indicated that he was a boxer, but whether he ever existed was something I never learned. Pether Maher, except for the picture, might well have been Master McGrath for all I knew, but the picture, on Jack's mantelpiece, was his pride and joy. Running a close second was his bird – one of the feathered kind: his wife saw to that – for Jack was a bird fancier and the house always held one in a cage, sometimes a canary, but more often a goldfinch.

Fairly regularly, he took me on the top of the open tram to the end of the route at the junction of Swords Road and Griffith Avenue where now stands the Garda Barracks, on Sunday mornings. He was going to catch finches, he told

9

Nellie, and indeed, sometimes he did, laying his lime traps up there at the Thatch where there was a football ground and a pub.

His wife, my grannie, Nellie, being older and wiser in her generation than I was, must have seen through him, but I looked forward to the excursions, walking up the narrow road, bordered by blackberry bushes, from Griffith Avenue to the Thatch, which now stands just above Collins Avenue, dancing along hand in hand with him, entranced by his tales of Pether Maher and his descriptions of the birds. When he trapped a finch or two, he'd sell them in the Bird Market in Francis Street, which was another big adventure, but half-way through the Sunday, Jack would abandon his bird hunt and repair to the Thatch. Maybe it was a shebeen, or maybe our crazy drinking laws deemed it a "bona-fide", but Jack got sufficient lubrication inside, and from him I learned the art of patience, cultivated later by a series of other instructors and instructresses, for not if I live to be a hundred years can I hope to count the hours I spent outside pubs while my grandda, maternal grandmother, or grand-aunt, or some other ageing boozer used me as an excuse to go "for a walk". My reward for being an alibi was a packet of arrowroot biscuits and a glass of raspberry, and I was venal enough to be bribed with the biscuits and the raspberry, for I knew that on the way home there'd be a penny hush money.

And as soon as I'd led my minder home and mutely confirmed his story, however implausible and unlikely, I'd have my nose pressed against the window of Bert Masterson's shop, mouth watering and penny clutched firmly in grubby fingers, spending a long time making the decision between Nutty Favourites, 6 for 1d, Peggy's Leg 1d each, Liquorice Laces 1d each, Nancy Balls 12 for 1d or Lucky Balls 1d each, and you might be lucky enough to find 1d stuck in the middle of the Lucky Ball. Only on your First Communion or Confirmation day would you be in a position to consider Scots Clan Chocolate Toffee, 4 for 1d, for 1d was a lot of money, even for exotic sweets.

Gur cake I didn't like a lot, though it was a favourite with most of the nearly always hungry kids and we got a fairsized chunk of it for a ha'penny, but unless it had the sickly pink icing, my gourmet's palate rejected it. Some of the older kids, about nine or ten, had, to my mind, inexplicable tastes, for instead of Nutty Favourites, 6 a 1d, they wasted their substance on a ha'penny Woodbine and a match.

Across the street from Bert's were Dixon's and Donnelly's, two side-by-side shops bearing the proud legend above their portals, "Fruiterer", and if Ruby, the daughter, was serving in Donnelly's, or May the daughter serving in Dixon's, we sidled in for a ha'porth of damaged fruit and e'er a straw rope. The straw ropes came to the shops bound around the fruit crates and we needed them, not for hanging anyone, even effigies, assuming we had known what they were, but for tying on lampposts as swings, our own pitiful merry-go-rounds.

The damaged fruit, apples, bananas, plums, oranges, was well bruised, but you got a good-sized parcel of it, and like the biscuit advertised on television, when the damage was scraped away, it fed a multitude.

It's only in the last ten years or so that I've come to realise we were deprived, and consequently should have been getting privileged treatment by the polis and the courts, but they mustn't have known the word either, or if they did, they did nothing about it, for the polis, always it seemed huge brooding men of fearsome mien, chased us with the zeal of the FBI after Dillinger. With a foot in the arse, or a belt of a massive glove across the head, they dispensed swift justice to the juvenile delinquent who played football on the street with a bundle of papers tied with string, or who swung on straw ropes out of lampposts or played kick-the-can, or hoppin-cock-arooshie on one foot across the breadth of Dorset Street, dodging the infrequent trams and the plentiful bicycles, as the opponent tried to shoulder you out of the game.

Thinking back on it, I know now I was born twenty years too early. Today's delinquents are appreciated.

Relievo was a favourite game, particularly at night when only the main street was lighted by the electric and the side streets by dim gas lights. Billy with the Lamplight came around every night with a long wand which he poked into the gas globe and then behold there was light – of a sort. For Relievo, sides were picked and the steps in front of Wynne's bootmaker's shop became the den. One team was out and the other had to capture them and confine them in the den. If one of the "outs" could run through the den shouting "Relievo", the captives could make their escape.

Being small and timid, I devised a means of never being caught. When we were out, I simply ignored the boundaries and window-shopped my way up Dorset Street to Frederick Street, and by the time I returned, the game was over.

Winters, were always cold. A lot of the youngsters were dressed in "police" clothes, a coarse navy blue gansey and brown corduroy shorts, and many went barefoot, presumably because there was no organisation to provide them with boots. Many were nearly barefoot, but escaped the stigma by getting, somehow, a pair of runners. We Kellys never had to wear the police clothes, although I was quite taken by them, yet I will never forget the terrible agonies I suffered one winter through having to wear a pair of trousers cut down from Free State Army bullswool. They chaffed the insides of my knees terribly and since no one wore underpants, they also left their mark on my crotch, thankfully without any permanent damage.

The remedy for the chaffing was Vaseline which gave some relief when I was in bed, but lost its effectiveness once the bullswool came in contact with my tender skin next day.

The penny tin of Vaseline, the penny tin of pink antiseptic ointment, the penn'orth of iodine and Mrs. Cullen's Powders were the complete pharmacopaeia of Dublin. For a cut or graze, the antiseptic ointment did the job; for coughs, colds, sore throats and sprains, the affected part was painted with the magic iodine. Mrs Cullen came to the aid of those afflicted with headache or toothache; and Vaseline was used for everything from sunburn to consumption.

There was no shortage of consumption – and why should there be? Not enough food, no hygiene, no proper clothing and damn little fresh air provided ideal breeding conditions for the bug. Not a month went by without somebody in the neighbourhood dying from consumption and you could always tell by the plumes on the horses in the hearse if the deceased was young or old. White was for the young and single, and black for the old and married.

Immediately after the hearse came the "moaning" coach, a cab with polished paintwork carrying the next of kin, and the remainder of the cortege was composed of a motley assortment of cabs or outside cars, hacks as they were called, the state of which was determined by the price the sympathisers could afford. And there was always a couple of young fellows scutting on the axles of the cab, determined to pay their respects, though they couldn't pay for the seats in the cortege.

No matter how poor, the deceased had to have a wake with saucers of snuff and plenty of porter, and the local publican supplied the booze on tick and often the funeral money until the insurance man turned up. Judging by the profits left in their wills by today's publicans, that tradition hasn't lasted in Dublin. The wake lasted long into the night and after a short break during which the decencies were observed in Glasnevin, were resumed in the Brian Boru on the return journey.

I'll always remember the first funeral I attended. I reckon I was about five years old and as a special treat I was allowed to ride with the jarvey on his box seat. He must have been one of our innumerable distant relations, many of whom had the most exciting of callings: bookmakers, jarveys, steeplejacks and the like. Not one of them, however, was other than poor.

A coming event must have thrown its shadow even then, for the funeral was to Kilbarrack where many years later I came to live. In the district, of course, not the graveyard, where is buried the Sham Squire, Francis Higgins, or at least his grave was visible when I came to the district. Also buried there are a convent of nuns, and Frank Flood, a nineteen-year-old lieutenant in the IRA who was hanged by the British in March 1921 for shooting Black and Tans.

The graveyard has one other claim to fame. Next door to it is the residence of one David Guiney, yet another Corkman whose proudest boast is that he comes from Cork, but like all the other Corkmen in Dublin evinces no interest whatever in returning to his native soil. He achieved some little fame in pitching or putting an enormous weight on various athletic fields and represented his country in the Olympic Games in 1948. There's quite a story attached to that, but it's his for the telling, not mine.

But back, many years, to my first funeral. After the

traditional three trips around the block, a custom having its origin I believe in the trí coiscéim na marbh of long ago, the cortege wended its way out to the country, down Richmond Road through Fairview and out the leafy sparsely built Howth Road till it reached Raheny. Raheny was a little rural village in those days and there was a big open space in front of one of the two pubs, no doubt specially arranged for parking of cabs and hacks on the way from funerals. The procession halted there – on the way out. Glasnevin funerals halted at the Brian Boru on the return journey, but apparently the mourners and the jarveys couldn't continue the hazardous journey through Indian country – there were another two miles to cover – without sustenance. I was lifted down from my perch and provided with the inevitable arrowroot biscuits and raspberry cordial and let stand in the porch for what seemed an interminable time.

The old people in the village of Raheny still tell the story, reputed to be true, of the two men who forgot the corpse. In the twenties and indeed much later, stillborn infants were wrapped in white cloth, and carried to the cemetery at an early hour and either thrown or lifted over the wall and left on the ground for the gravediggers to bury. It saved the price of a funeral and a grave, and God knew, many people went into debt for years to bury their grown-ups.

At any rate, local folklore has it that these two men were carrying an infant to the graveyard, but to fortify themselves for the task and the remainder of the journey, repaired to the pub on the way out.

The barman, susceptible to the sensitivities of the other customers, took the tiny bundle from the bar and put it underneath the counter. And, so the story goes, after the funeral men had had a few snorthers, they set off for

Kilbarrack Graveyard, leaving the pitiful bundle in the pub. It was only when they reached their destination they remembered the reason for their journey.

Nothing like that, so far as I can recall, took place with our obsequies, and the corpse was disposed of with decorum, but the Raheny tavern was revisited on the return journey and profited considerably. Once the corpse had been interred, the centrepoint of the affair switched to the living, for, as is the wont with funerals the attenders feel they have to celebrate simply because they are still alive. This is the difference between funerals and weddings, for funerals generate laughter, while weddings induce tears.

Once more, I was stuffed with biscuits and cordials and on the eight miles journey back to the street, slept contentedly beside the tipsy jarvey, under the smelly horse blanket which covered his knees when the horse didn't need it.

There's an old saying, "you might as well sing grief as cry it," so perhaps it's not surprising that music and song formed a big part of that Dublin life. The first song I remember is "Keep the Home Fires Burning" sung by my mother as a lullaby for some of the younger kids, and whenever I see *The Plough and the Stars* and hear that line, I'm transported back a half century in time. Hooleys were more frequent than would be imagined in a poverty-stricken area, so the booze must have been cheap or maybe the people had their priorities right. A christening or the departure of someone to seek work in England was a fitting occasion for a hooley, as was a wedding, which quite often was followed by the introduction of a new citizen in a remarkably short time. But, sure, the people had to have some pastime.

We kids weren't allowed into the hooleys, but we crept up the dark stairs and huddled outside the doors listening to the singing and the melodeon or the concertina being squeezed in accompaniment. Molly, a little hunchback with glasses and nothing else to recommend her except a good untrained voice always rendered "By the Bright Silvry Li . . . hite of the Moon" as the highlight of the hooley.

And the young men, many back from the First War, penniless and tobacco-less, could afford to do nothing except gather in groups of up to thirty at night, standing at the street corners, singing. Just singing. You might as well sing hopelessness as cry it, I suppose.

Kids didn't feel the hopelessness. I suppose they were shielded from it, to a large degree by their parents, and also by the natural concentration they have on the now, rather than the morrow. Not having anything, we missed nothing, for, as they say, what you never had you'll never miss. Yet, money could be made. There was a shop in Capel Street which bought and sold second-hand books and comics and it was surprising how many copies of the *Magnet*, the *Gem, Film Fun, Rover, Wizard* and *Hotspur* could be picked up and sold for a ha'penny. Jack the Rag pushing his three-wheeler skip offered air balloons for jam jars, and sometimes he'd buy jam jars 1d for the pound pot and 1d for the pound jar. He must have had some way of making money from them, or he wouldn't have been so generous. The forerunner of the giant chains in the ice-cream business was the ice-cream man who signalled his coming by blowing a horn. He usually had a gaudily painted hand cart, adapted to hold the zinc bucket of ice-cream around which was packed block ice. For a ha'penny you could have a cornet or half a wafer, and if you hadn't a ha'penny, he might give you a piece of ice to suck, which was the next best thing. And in Dublin then, you learned very quickly to accept the next best thing. If you could get it.

We didn't need a lot of money for entertainment. Discos, television, even the wireless were in the realms of science fiction, so in summer we swam in the Canal at the second lock up from Binn's Bridge, ignoring the dead dogs or pushing them out of the way. Those who couldn't swim learned to keep afloat by tying two paraffin oil tins with a piece of twine and lying on the twine while learning. It was a notably cheap form of waterwings, though somewhat hazardous since the rolled paper corks in the tins came loose at awkward moments. But we had no fatalities, and sometimes, when the mood of adventure was on us, we walked to Dollymount and back. If we were lucky, we got two pieces of bread and butter, or more often, marge, for our day's rations.

There was also the Phoenix Park, a wonderland to countless generations of Dubliners. We walked up the North Circular Road, past Harry Briggs' garage, selling R.O.P petrol at ten pence a gallon, passed Mountjoy Police Station and the prison, outside which we always blessed ourselves for Kevin Barry, and hurried past. Then, in the Park, Jimmy and Noel and I left the dirty streets behind us and entered the world of Deerfoot the Pawnee roaming the praries, outwitting the savage Apache or Sioux as we guided imaginary troops of white men across the trackless plains. Deerfoot books were very popular, though today I suspect he'd be regarded as a Red Uncle Tom by the American Indians.

Any rale Dubalanman will tell you the people were great in them days. And he'll be right, for there was a spirit of comradeship in misery which transcended the conditions, and neighbourliness wasn't just something that sociologists prated about. It was practised every day and if a neighbour was in trouble the others, no matter how little they had, went short to help out. And the shopkeepers helped. Tommy in Daly's

(Grocer and Purveyor) always picked the least cracked of the 4d a dozen cracked eggs for his customers, and Harry, in Logan's (General Grocer) always slipped in a rasher or two in the 6d a pound pieces of bacon.

Ruby Donnelly and May Dixon, the aforementioned daughters of shopkeepers, always tried to slip in a whole apple or orange in the ha'porth of damaged fruit, and poor Bert Masterson couldn't have died rich. He kept the little general store at the corner, and all his customers were "on the book", a penny notebook in which he entered every item purchased on credit for settlement at the end of the week. At the end of the week he usually had to write the magic words "Bal car fwd". I bet Thomas Lipton or Galen Weston never did that, and at Christmas Bert gave all his customers a fruity brack, a Christmas candle, and a half bottle of Old Tawny Wine, a potion of uncertain origin which nonetheless passed the test of the local connoisseurs.

Characters there were in plenty. Unlike today when affluence and suburbanisation has imposed a grey standard of anonymity and conformity, the streets of Dublin then were thronged with them. A lady in a shawl played the banjo and did a step dance outside Bill Bushe's pub a couple of times a week. She knew only one tune, "Mick McGilligan's Daughter, Maryanne", which was the only name by which she was identified. She wasn't mad, but Cappo was. He had a white beard and his coat was fastened with a light rope, and he wandered the streets with a crucifix in his hands blessing everybody, irrespective of creed or position. It didn't do one damn bit of harm either, though it may not have done any good. He was mad, the oul' wans said, religious mad, and that was the worst form. So too, they claimed was Matt Talbot "wrappin' chains around himself and kneelin' for hours in the chapel". My mother, God rest her, spoke little about Matt, except to endorse the general view, and family folklore has it that he was a relation of a third or maybe it was a fourth cousin of ours, which would explain her reticence, since if people knew, they might suspect the strain ran in the family.

Hot Potato was a smallish inoffensive ruddy-faced man who walked the streets minding his own business, respectably dressed in a black overcoat and wearing a bowler hat. He kept himself to himself. Until somebody shouted "Hot potato", whereupon he raged into attempted assault on whoever had shouted. Maybe he had been hypnotised and those were the keywords? Otherwise his behaviour was inexplicable, because we often lit fires in the back lanes, throwing potatoes into them until they were burned black and covered with soot. Then we ate them. They tasted lovely too.

Dingers lived up the lane. He was the companion and minder of a well-known lady of the night and day, and he was a hard man. 'Twas said that when he had no money and needed a drink, he'd walk into the pub and spit into the nearest pint on the counter. If the owner objected he'd get a punch that would fell him, and Dingers would drink the pint. If the owner didn't object, Dingers drank the pint and left him alone. I once saw the peelers arresting him and bringing him up the North Circular Road to Mountjoy station. It took six big DMP men and they had to cut his belt and let his trousers drop around his ankles before they could manage it.

Maybe ten or twelve years later, five of us from the club were having a co-operative pint in the former McAuley's pub when Dingers came in looking for free drink. He bumped against Dick spoiling for a row, but the years had caught up with him. With as sweet a right uppercut as I've seen outside the ring, Dick floored him.

By a peculiar coincidence, Terry and I were coming from work about 11 p.m. and as we passed through Summerhill, Dinger's lady was sitting on a step, she wrapped in a shawl, her hand wrapped about a wine bottle. She asked us did we want to do business. I felt a strange sort of sadness for the two of them. Escape from the environment was, I should imagine, on everyone's mind all the time.

My avenue was my imagination. When I was dispatched to Rourke's Bakery all the way down in Store Street, for a sackful of split loaves and thruppence worth of fancy bread, I wasn't walking the length of Gardiner Street, past the pawn shop which saw the women twice a week, on Saturdays to redeem the man's suit or the woman's wedding ring, and on Mondays to put them in again, though the wedding ring was always last to go. Nor was I passing the Jesuit Church from which the priests often emerged and they wearing the flat Spanish hats that the Dicky Ministers wore, nor Killane's pub at the corner of Parnell Street, nor the remnants of Monto on the left-hand side.

I wasn't trotting along those streets. I was on a daring mission through the burning desert for the Foreign Legion, dodging the merciless Arabs, thousands of whom lined the route. And on the way home, I was again dodging them, though they were in hot pursuit, as I brought the supplies to the beleaguered fort. I always got through. That's why the commandant always picked me.

Nowadays, I'd probably be regarded as a spacer, and sent for assessment by a juvenile psychiatrist, who'd recommend that I be given a lorry-load of sand and as many figs as I could eat.

Once, in second class in Plás Mhuire, the brudder, in one of his rare attempts to communicate and bridge the generation gap, asked me what I did when I went home after school. Ever truthful, I told him I played with a hoop. He looked at me wonderingly, as if I had just confirmed his long held suspicion that I was mentally retarded, and drily asked: "Aren't you a bit old for that?" I was eight.

For my part, I was confirmed in my belief that he, like all adults, was incredibly stupid. He should have known that my hoop was an aeroplane.

A tyre-covered bicycle wheel-rim was a Spad, a Fokker triplane, a Nieuport or an Albatross, depending on which side I was helping to win the Great War in the air at the time. A motor cycle rim was a Bristol Fighter or a Rumpler; and a car tyre was a D.H.9 or a Gotha. He didn't know! And he trying to teach us, with his "Má tá Gaeilge agat, labhair í"!

Envy, I knew from my penny catechism, was one of the seven deadly sins but I didn't recognise it, although now I know it was the emotion I felt on autumn Sunday evenings, just as the Angelus bell was ringing as I hurried home from the Botanic Gardens down through Iona Road with the dusk and a wispy mist on that deserted road emphasising the difference between the privacy and security of the suburbs and the noise and overcrowding of Dorset Street.

From the redbrick houses, behind drawn curtains, came the tinkling of pianos, borne, it seemed, on the rays of electric light which filtered through chinks in the drapes. And the yearning I felt was envy, though I didn't know, envy for a life secure and ordered and safe and a house which was occupied by only one family, a house where there could be a bit of privacy.

In 1930 it happened. Daddy, who had had a succession of short-term, drudging jobs since he came out of the Army Air Corps two years earlier, got a permanent and well-paying job, and we got a house of our own. With a bathroom and toilet and hot and cold running water. With enough space that we could live only two to each room. With the electric and the wireless. I entered a new world.

In the first thirty years of this century Dublin didn't change much. It changed a lot in the next thirty, and a lot more in the following fifteen. The people changed, the scene changed.

Now, when I'm coming home, over Dublin Bay and the pilot announces "We're approaching Dublin", I look down and see the ugliness of Liberty Hall, Hawkins House and the other glass and concrete monstrosities which emphasise the beauty of the Custom House, and the streets through which the thugs, the hopheads, the muggers, the gunmen and the murderers roam at will, I scream silently, "That is not Dublin. There is no longer a Dublin. Me darlin' Dublin's dead and gone."

Chapter 2

The Judas Link

Judas Iscariot, the most infamous traitor in the history of the world, was lost to the Church because of thirty pieces of silver. So was I, for the same amount. But Iscariot got his thirty pieces of silver, and my defection, or rather, my absence from active involvement in the Church for the past thirty years or so can be attributed to the lack of thirty pieces of silver.

Judas Iscariot has always been a fascinating character to me. I could never figure out why he betrayed his Master, why he had to put the finger on Jesus, who must have been a familiar figure to the Romans and the Jews who wanted him. Every time his name comes to mind I make a note to investigate the reasons behind his betrayal of Our Lord but I never get around to it. I know that the Prophecy had to be fulfilled, according to the teaching of one of our Christian Brothers beyond in Plas Mhuire at the Black Church many years ago, and that Christ had to die to redeem the world. Nevertheless, I still haven't found out why Judas became the traitor of all time.

He was one of the disciples and had he not betrayed his Master, he would have become one of the first bishops of the Church, possibly a martyr, and most probably a Saint. I, on the other hand, might well have gone on to become a priest, a parish priest, a bishop, archbishop or cardinal, had my parents been able to spare thirty pieces of silver in the early thirties. They didn't, so I became what I am, and many people have their own opinions as to what that is.

The seeds of my religion were sown at an early stage in my life. At the age of four I was committed to the care of the Sisters of Charity in the convent school in Gardiner Street. Though it may be thought nowadays that four is a bit early to be sent to school, it was the common thing in the Dublin of fifty years ago, when every mother in the poorer parts of the city was like the old woman who lived in a shoe: she had so many children she didn't know what to do. So as soon as they could walk, children were sent to school, giving relief to the mothers who often had younger children in the home.

I can remember the teachers in that little school – Sister Dorothy the Head, Mrs Flood, Miss Barnwell, Miss Sharpe and Miss Richardson – as well as some of my schoolmates, Peter Keeley who made his name as a footballer, Pat Owens, well known in the GAA publishing world and John McGauran who won a few titles as an amateur boxer.

It was a typical convent school, with plenty of hymns and prayers interspersed with lessons in sums, readin' and ritin', and it was Miss Sharpe who conferred on me the greatest boon in my life, when she taught me to read. She even bought, specially for me, a children's comic called *Chicks' Own*, in which the words were broken up to help little ones learn to read.

Sister Dorothy, as may be expected, took care of our religious education, which also involved trooping us up the lane to St Francis Xavier Church in Gardiner Street for the Holy Hour and Benediction. Whatever about Archbishop

Lefebvre's excesses, I have never lost my love for the majesty and solemnity of the Tridentine ceremonials.

Gardiner Street church, as it was known locally, will always hold a special place in my heart. At Benediction, the sweet sickly smell of incense, the blaze of the candles on the high altar, reflected by the oil paintings of great Jesuits – Xavier dying at Samoa or wherever it was, Ignatius of Loyola, Blessed Claude de la Columbière – the side altars, the boom of the organ and the children piping "Holy God, we praise Thy name" and "Tantum Ergo", as well as "Oh, Mother Eye" (as we thought it was), all implanted in me a sense of mystery which can never be eradicated.

From the convent, I went to Plás Mhuire, where again Religious Knowledge and ritual were part of our life. The May Altar for Our Lady was always decorated with flowers and candles – after all, she was the patron saint of the school – and the choir, taught by Mrs Boylan, which cleaned up at the Feis Ceoil every year, was pressed into service each afternoon in May. Again, "Oh, Mother Eye" was high on the list of hymns, as was "Hail Queen of Heaven," which we sang to the accompaniment of the harmonium.

At that time, on Holy Thursdays it was obligatory to "do" the Seven Chapels, which involved visiting seven churches and reciting prayers in each of them to gain indulgences; we trudged all over the city to visit our seven chapels. They were known as "chapels" in Dublin, to distinguish them from "churches" which had to be Protestant, and the way you knew a non-Catholic, in our circles, was by his statement that he went to church on Sundays, when the rest of us went to Mass in the chapel.

It's not to be wondered at, then, that I entertained serious thoughts of the priesthood when I was about ten or eleven. A lot of the boys in Plás Mhuire served Mass: my inseparable pals, Jimmy Gough, who died later in the British Air Force during the War, and Noel Kearney, who also served in the Air Force but survived the War, were amongst them.

Jimmy served Mass in the chapel attached to the Mater Hospital, and when there was a vacancy for an altar boy he urged me to volunteer. I knew the Latin responses to the Mass – we all had to learn them as part of the Catechism – and I could "Introibo ad altare Dei" with the best of them. Besides, Jimmy added, you always got your breakfast after Mass, rasher and egg and sausage, as well as tea and bread and butter. As we were lucky if we had either a rasher or an egg for breakfast on Sundays, this was a powerful inducement, and as the commercial has it, the butter was the cream, since most of the week when Dad was out of work Maypole Maggie Ryan (10d a pound) was the normal condiment.

It was enough to turn my dormant fervour for the Church into a blazing fire, and I couldn't wait for three o'clock to get out of school and tell them at home. At the door, I told Jimmy I'd ask me ma, and helter-skelter down the steps I dashed, schoolbag banging on my backside as I skidded around the corner into Dorset Street, with the Plaza on my right, past the chipper where we could buy a penn'orth of chips when we were in funds, past Brogan's, the shop which sold Indian Ale out of a barrel at a ha'penny a glass, past Kennedy's Bakery, past all the shops without the usual nose-pressing against the windows which normally attended our dilatory home-going.

Panting from excitement and exertion, I burst in the door. My mother, with one of the smaller children tugging at her skirt, was busy about her housework. As I flung my schoolbag into the corner, she asked: "What has you home so early with your breath in your fist? Is it the police chasing you or what?"

"Mother," I babbled, "I'm goin' to be an altar boy – in the Mater. With Jimmy. An' we'll get our breakfast every mornin' after Mass. They'll take me. An' I know the prayers."

Absently she answered: "Shure that's a good thing and it won't do you a bit of harm in the world. But if they're waiting for you to serve six Mass, the priest'll have to be doing it on his own."

Young as I was, I knew instinctively that I now had come to Becher's Brook. "Mother, I'll need a surplus."

"Well, that's no bother. You can use Jack's that he got for his Sodality. I'll put a tuck in it if it's too big."

"Mother, I'll need one of these black things that the Brothers wear, a sootan."

"We haven't got one of them."

"No, I know, but . . ." I faltered . . . "they're only thirty bob. . ." my voice died away. So did my hopes, as I looked at her face.

Thirty bob would feed the family for a week, she told me gently, and her face crumpled. With her husband out of work and six children to feed, a soutane was the last of a long long list of needs in the Kelly household.

And that's how my link with Judas was established.

Chapter 3

The Knife

Friends, acquaintances and enemies of mine have claimed on occasion that I'm a bit of an odd-ball. On being pressed, they may sometimes concede that they think I'm a bit mad in the head, as distinct from being mad from drink for which there is a cure. I don't agree with them, and, unlike that French fellow who said he mightn't agree with them, but he would defend to the death their right to their own opinion, I have no intention of defending their rights to the death or to anything else. I will, however, allow anybody the right to his own opinion, and go my own way. "Live and let live" is my motto, and if people don't agree with me, well, that's their hard luck.

Nevertheless, if there is a grain of truth in their assessment, a couple of incidents in my childhood could be responsible, and I have no doubt that if I were daft enough, or rich enough, or idle enough to lie on a couch and pay a psychiatrist enormous sums of money for listening to recollections of my childhood, he could excuse my present aberrations on the grounds that my mind has been affected by my early experiences.

In that year of grace, 1932, the year of the Eucharistic

Congress, I was ten years old and a pupil at Plás Mhuire C.B.S. That's the one beside the Black Church where, if you run around it three times at midnight, you'll see the divil. Four of us, greatly daring, did it once. I got a stitch in my side because we ran like hell, and a hiding from my father when I got home for being out so late. But around the Black Church we saw nothing. At that time I dearly wanted to be a Boy Scout. Possibly it was because of living in a crowded slum area that I yearned for the open air and the freedom of spaces, but in any event I couldn't join the Scouts until I was eleven.

I couldn't join the Cubs because I didn't know where they hung out, and anyway the Cubs were kid stuff. Undersized, pale and skinny, nevertheless I trailed after, rather than with, a gang of big fellows, aged thirteen or fourteen, from Synnott Place, and two of them, Simon and Dicky, were particularly kind to me. They were also Scouts, arms laden with merit badges, and Dicky was an APL. For the edification of those of you who have never had the benefit of scouting, an APL was, and presumably still is, an assistant patrol leader, *so,* in my eyes, Dicky was a worthy object of admiration. I pestered them so much, that they eventually capitulated and brought me to the Scouts' Hall in Phibsboro, where, to my unbounded joy, the Scoutmaster who was obviously a good-natured person, "enrolled" me in the troop and allocated me to the Lion Patrol. I didn't know then, nor did I know until the troop was disbanded twelve months later, that I was never officially a Scout, though during my active service, I partook in all the activities, including marches through the city, church parades and camps. The Scoutmaster let me string along as an unofficial supernumerary, since he couldn't register me at HQ because I was under age. Many years later, long after the troop had been disbanded for a dark and hush-hush reason, which,

I gather, would have delighted the scavenging reporters of the *News of the World*, I fully appreciated the thoughtfulness of the man in enabling a little boy to achieve his ambition and thus preventing heartbreak.

So there I was – a Scout. There was only one dark cloud on the horizon. I had to attend parades in civvies. I didn't have a uniform, and since the uniform cost twenty-five bob, I had no prospect of getting one, though when my mother at last had to buy me socks, I prevailed on her to buy black ones. Even then, they weren't the all-black Scouts' socks: they had two green rings around the top. Utility socks, they might be called, for as well as serving as everyday wear, they were just the job for scouting, and they trebled as football socks when needed.

Although all my life I have never had wealth, and I never will, somehow there was always a guardian angel who looked after me, and after about two months of scouting, Batty Ball, who lived in the North Circular Road, a few doors down from the house in which Sean O'Casey had lived, took pity on me, and sold me a Scout's trousers, shirt and belt for half-a-crown. He threw in a hat, too, which, though it fitted fairly well with a rolled newspaper inside the band, would never be other than shapeless. It did serve one purpose, however. As I ironed and brushed it continually and wore it proudly, it afforded hours of surreptitious and free amusement for my mother and grandmother who never failed to hang out of the window to see me march to parades.

Georgie Wynne, the bootmaker next door, who had been in the Baden Powell Scouts – so you can guess his religion – gave me a stave. It was six feet long, and like Ulick O'Connor's vaulting pole, completely unmanageable, especially by a boy half its height. Scouts' staves, like the knives which open cans and take stones out of horses' hooves, can be used, in theory, for many things. They said you could tie them together to build a bridge over a river or use them as the frame for a shelter if you were caught out on the moors at night. (I never saw a moor to this day.) By turning an overcoat a certain way, the stave could be used as a stretcher, or when climbing up sheer surfaces, a Scout could lower his stave and help his comrades up. How he was to get to the top was never explained, and I never saw a stave used for any of those purposes, though we did learn a sort of arms drill with them. To the disgust of my fellows, I never got out of the habit of referring to my stave as my "Scout's pole".

The neckerchief by which the troop is identified, presented no problem. Ours was red and blue, so my grannie got from somewhere a piece of red cloth and a piece of blue cloth and stitched them together to make two neckerchiefs. They were much smaller than the official issue and of a slightly different hue, but that was not a consideration which weighed with me. I, in my own tiny mind, was a Scout, fully-fledged and fully-uniformed.

There was only one thing I lacked: a sheath-knife. My father, God rest his soul, scraped up half-a-crown and bought me a folding knife which had one large blade, and a pointed yoke which some held was for splicing ropes, others that it was for taking stones out of horses' hooves, and still others maintained that it was for digging handholes in rocky mountain faces. I used it for putting holes in the cans of condensed milk we used on camps, for which purpose it was very effective. The knife clipped on to a hook on my belt, and it was counterbalanced on the other side by a whistle. It was great. But it wasn't a sheath-knife. They cost, at the time, from 7/6d upwards, so the future stretched bleak and sheath-knifeless in front of me.

Until September, when we had our first camp, or at least my first camp, for a number of the troop were experienced campers. We went to Lord Holmpatrick's estate in Abbotstown, near Blanchardstown, then miles out in the country, now the site of the James Connolly Hospital. I thoroughly enjoyed the camp and in the near half-century since then, I have never completely lost my love for camping. At our first parade after the camp, the Scoutmaster announced an essay competition on "My First Camp" and, incredibly, the prize for the best essay was to be . . . a sheath-knife!

Even at that age I was a good writer. Fed on a literary diet of the *Rover, Hotspur, Wizard, Wings, Air Aces, War Hawks, William* and *The Saint,* and possessed of a lively imagination, I spurned the conventional "Our first camp was a wonderful affair" approach, and wrote a good essay in a humorous vein. And it was no surprise to me when the scoutmaster announced that the best essay had been produced by Scout William Kelly.

I stepped forward briskly, came to attention, and gave him the three-fingered salute, fingers to the brim of the hat. Bursting with pride and joy, I could barely control myself from snatching the sheath-knife from the table.

But pride then, as always, went before a fall.

The Scoutmaster said: "Scout Kelly's essay was far and away the best."

My short and discoloured neckerchief rose perceptibly as my narrow chest filled with vainglory.

The Scoutmaster bent towards me and said: "It was so good, that I can't believe you didn't have help in doing it."

I flushed and stammered: "I didn't, sir, I did it myself, sir."

Gently, he said: "Have you a big brother? What class is he in?"

Shy, confused and frustrated, I stuttered: "He's in first year, sir, but he didn't help me."

Softly and somewhat sadly, he said: "I'm sorry, the essay is too advanced to have been written by a boy of ten, so I'm awarding the first prize to Patrol Leader Flood. But as a consolation prize, I'm giving you this watch . . ."

I'd never had a watch in my life. And this was a good-sized strong pocket watch with a healthy tick. But it wasn't a sheath-knife. I was too young and uncertain, as well as bewildered, to take umbrage at the slur on my honesty. The two-fingered salute hadn't been invented then or I might have been tempted to use it. Instead, I unbuttoned the flap and put the watch in my breast pocket, managed a salute and a sharp about-turn and fled down the hall, tears streaming down my face, past the Lion Patrol, the Owl Patrol, the Otter Patrol, all the patrols drawn up in formation, out through the gate of St Peter's School, down past the church, past Doyle's Corner, past Mountjoy Jail, not forgetting in all my misery to bless myself for Kevin Barry, past Leo Street, and St Benedict's Garden's, past Shiels' Garage, and Lynch's Dairy and Cahill's Chemist's, charged through the hall and up the stairs to throw myself on the bed where I sobbed the whole night long.

Chapter 4

"There's no Ghosts, only the Holy Ghost"

Johnny Leonard lived in the parlour of No. 85 and he was much older than I at the time I'm speaking about. He must have been about fourteen, for every now and again he was in business, driving an ass and cart in his various enterprises, and we liked him, for, unlike the other big fellows, he didn't bully us five and six-year-olds. I don't know if Johnny is alive or dead now, as it's half a century since I saw him and his importance in my life then was that he saw the Banshee sitting on the window sill the night his mother died. She was a little old woman dressed all in black, he said, with long black hair and glowing eyes, and she keened as Mrs. Leonard breathed her last. The Banshee threw her comb at him, Johnny vowed, but fortunately the window was closed and Johnny lived, for had the comb struck him, he would have gone along with his mother. He was the only one I knew who had seen the Banshee and lived to tell the tale, though my grandmother who came from the wilds of the back of County Galway knew all about Banshees, Féar Gorta, Jack O' Lanterns and the rest of the myriad spirits which wandered around Ireland mid-way through the third decade of this century. By the light of her paraffin oil lamp in her lonely room she used to tell me all about them, especially when she didn't have a novel to read, for she was a great reader, forever despatching me to the library and the second-hand bookshops to get her a Charles Garvice, an Ethel M. Dell, or a Ruby M. Ayres. Ghosts were as real to the two of us as we were ourselves, and a number of the natives of Dorset Street, if they didn't believe in ghosts, didn't take any chances. They avoided certain places after dark. The Lucky Lane between Sinnott Place and the North Circular Road was known to be haunted, as was the lane up at the back of the Mater Hospital, where the dead house used to be. Everyone knew that, and it wasn't any great surprise, because the electric was only on the main road and the sparse gas lamps threw a sickly circle of dim light which barely eased the darkness of the winter's nights. Everyone knew that ghosts preferred the darkness, which was why we huddled on the stairs together after Harry Laffan's magic lantern shows had ended and the candle had gone out, telling ourselves, "There's no ghosts only the Holy Ghost", before racing wildly home.

There was more hope than faith in the incantation and the panting dash up the unlit four flights of stairs to the safety of home was as terrifying to me as the crossing of the Styx was to whoever crossed it and came back to tell the tale. These old houses – old, it seemed, as time itself, and lived in by so many and diverse people – must have been the scene of some weird happenings in their varied history, and while I devoutly repeated "There's no ghosts only the Holy Ghost", I wasn't altogether convinced. In winter, or when the wind blew, they were full of sound, creaks and whispers, and it was easy to imagine strange spirits immured in the walls, bemoaning their fate, or seeking their release. Then, too, there was the picture on our wall, which from my bed was that of a malevolent old man with a white beard. Only when I was within six inches of it did it resolve itself into a scene of two men standing at a gate, with a white cloud in the background. Often, before I went to sleep, it would frighten me so much that I'd call for Mammy, and on learning what was wrong, she'd counsel me: "Say a Hail Mary, and it'll be alright."

As I grew up, I became less afraid of the other world, and not at all afraid of this one, because at that time in Dublin you didn't have to be afraid of unprovoked attack. If you minded your own business, you didn't get into fights.

And I was minding my own business that night in June 1940, as I was walking home very pleased with myself, having left my newest girl to her respectable door with the promise of a date later in the week. I walked up Griffith Avenue, enjoying the midnight moonlight which bathed the gardens of the trim suburban houses and reflected off the trees that marched straight as a file of soldiers all the way up to Ballymun. Although outside Ireland the world was busily engaged in ridding itself of millions of humans by use of a variety of barbaric weapons, war was far from my mind as I turned right into Grace Park Road. It wasn't dark, so I wasn't whistling and my footsteps echoed comfortingly off the footpath as I went by the wall of the convent which stretched all along the left-hand side up to Beaumont Road.

Unconsciously as I strolled, my mind, affected by the night, was tossing around "Moon, June, Dance, Romance", for the pop songs of that era had real words and music and they seemed very suited to my mood. Then, just as I came to the main gate of the convent, I felt a presence. There was no sound, just a feeling someone or something was coming behind me. Mugging hadn't been invented, and indeed in our lovely city then you could walk the length and breadth of it without being molested, at any time of the day or night. It didn't worry me unduly so I kept on. A few more yards and the feeling became more pronounced, making me feel a bit uneasy. There was nothing behind me, yet the feeling lingered. Another few yards, and I glanced around again. This time I saw it. It was a big black dog, about the size of a Labrador, padding along silently in my wake.

Since I'd always had some kind of dog, I felt distinctly relieved and I spoke to him stretching out my hand in the approved manner. As I stopped so did he. Well, I felt, if he's not in the mood for talking, he can do whatever dogs do when they're told to shag off, and on I went again. This time, I threw a glance over my shoulder, and the black dog was still there, though a chance ray of light on the far side of the road made his eyes glow red. A trick of light, I assured myself, and stepped up the pace just a bit, feeling by now that there was something definitely not right. Then it came to me. Though the dog was walking three or four yards behind me, there was not the slightest sound on the whole of Grace Park Road. Surely I should have heard the scrape of his claws, or, however faint, the pad of his paws? But there was nothing but silence, and me and the black dog, on the Grace Park Road. The houses, all on the far side of the road were comfortably shuttered against the night. Not a trace of wind disturbed the hedges. Hurrying just short of an undignified trot, for by now the memory of Johnny Leonard and my grandmother's stories had brushed all thoughts of "Moon, June, Dance and Romance" from my mind, I kept glancing over my shoulder. He was still there. And as we moved into the semi-dark between the streetlights, his eyes still glowed.

The junction with Collins Avenue was only about thirty yards away and the dog still followed, him never saying a word, about three yards behind me. I passed the pathetic little memorial which still marks the spot where Martin Hogan, a Republican, was found shot dead just before the end of the Civil War, in 1923. The dog never passed it. He vanished.

Brave now, I stood at the corner of Collins Avenue for about five minutes, my eyes searching the length of Grace Park Road which stretched away down from me, peaceful and sleeping. There was no sign of the dog. There was no sign of anything. I was alone.

I can offer no explanation. Sometimes, ghosts or spirits appear to give warning of some impending misfortune, but if the black dog was a warning, he was in the wrong place at the right time, for I sailed through the next few weeks in the best of form, and my new romance, like so many of them, blossomed for another while.

In Ireland, three is one of the mystical numbers, though I believe seven is the most popular in other lands. Here, the superstitious – and all Irish are superstitious whether or not they admit it – believe that happenings run in threes. If there's a death in your circle, they say, you'll hear of three. If someone of the family has a bit of ill fortune, two other bits will follow. I don't know if it holds for good fortune, never having had much experience of that commodity and I sincerely hope it doesn't hold for ghostly visitations. For I had my second supernatural experience inside the next two years, and it was far more terrifying, because it happened in my own house, where with all the prayers said, the holy water sprinkled, and the religious pictures and statues, there should have been no place more impregnable to spirits.

I had been asleep for an hour or so, when something wakened me. In the other bed, Jack's breathing was regular as he slept the sleep of the just, or the too-poor-to-be-otherwise, for that night at least. From being in a warm slumber, I was jerked awake, not by a noise or disturbance, simply by a feeling and immediately I was bathed in the cold sweat of sudden fear.

At the foot of my bed was a shapeless form of misty white light.

It had the contours of neither man nor beast, nor were there any defined lines. It looked rather like a smallish pillar of light, though the light wasn't bright nor was it transparent. There were no features, no arms, no legs. But it was a being, of that I am sure. For how long it remained at the foot of my bed, I do not know. I lay there paralysed with absolute and unutterable terror. Then slowly, very slowly, it made its way up the side of my bed, between mine and Jack's. He slept on, undisturbed, and I could still hear his measured breathing. But I could not move hand or foot, nor could I cry out. At the level of my chest it stopped. I thought my heart would burst from fear. In a passion of despair I somehow threw up my arms, the easier to fling myself out the window to get away from the apparition, and then it disappeared.

I was bathed in perspiration, trembling from head to foot, so badly I felt the whole room must be rocking. When I pressed the light switch all was normal in the room. My brother slept peacefully. The only trace of anything unusual was that the door which had been tightly closed, was ajar. Once more, I can offer no explanation. The few people to whom I related these events, either scoffed that I had indulged in too many spirits, or that the dog was real and the apparition a nightmare. But I know I was cold sober on both occasions, and the second experience, like the first, was not a portent of disaster, for my life went on in the normal way.

I have never possessed second sight, clairvoyance or extra sensory perception, indeed there are those who suggest I never possessed even common sense, and they might be right. Yet that area had been the site of some hideous murders. Down at the bottom of Grace Park Road, in Clonturk Park, two innocent young men had been taken from the Castle by the Auxiliaries and after buckets had been put over their heads, shot dead, in the mistaken belief they had been implicated in the shooting of spies by the I.R.A. on Bloody Sunday. At the upper end of Grace Park, Martin Hogan was shot to death during the Civil War and at Puckstown, which is now the Yellow Road, Alfie Cole and George Colley, two Republicans, were murdered by Free State soldiers, during that time.

And on Good Friday, one of the three cross days of the year, shortly after we had moved into Beaumont Road, a young motorcyclist was killed bloodily and instantly in a collision at the crossroads of Grace Park and Collins Avenue. Prior to 1939, the whole area had been "in the country", and who can tell what murders and other horrors took place there in the bad old days?

William Shakespeare believed in ghosts, as did William Butler Yeats, who claimed to have seen the Brown Boy in Oliver Gogarty's Renvyle House in Galway.

For the past forty years I have been untroubled by any but material things: rackrents, mortgages, taxes, illness and unreasonable people. Yet sometimes when the wind is keening around our little house, not too far from Kilbarrack Graveyard, I find myself mentally repeating, "There's no ghosts only the Holy Ghost", and I'm still not convinced.

Chapter 5

The Sporting Life (1)

It's the loneliest place in the world, the ring. You're completely on your own. No one can help you. And you can't get out of it. Of course you could make a dive between the ropes and run all the way up the hall to the dressing room, and although there's nothing you'd like better, somehow your legs won't do it. So you're stuck there in the corner.

The lights are hellishly bright over the twenty-foot square, but outside their arc it's all darkness except for the glowworms of cigarettes in ranks right up to the distant back wall, and all you can see is white blobs. It's hard to realise that the blobs are faces, fat, skinny, cruel or kind, all of them carrying one expression if you could only see it, reflecting the primeval anticipation of the meeting between hunter and hunted, with the certain knowledge that there can be only one winner.

Looking up at the lights hurts your eyes. They are shielded with deep cowls like the lights over a billiard table, only much bigger, and you can see thick clouds of tobacco smoke rising lazily into the cowls. I felt terribly lonely and wondered how in the name of God I'd let myself in for this ordeal.

It was a hundred years ago. I was about to make my debut as a pro – me, who had learned the rudiments of boxing in the Boy Scouts under Battling Brannigan and from cigarette pictures in which Ernie Smith, Dick Hearns and Andy Sharkey of the famous Garda boxing team demonstrated the various punches which were described on the back of the card in small print. Only ten months earlier I had become a foundation member of the local boxing club. With six other would-be boxers, I dug the foundations and helped erect the army hut which became the gym.

In the early days of the club we had Slogger as trainer. Slogger was fiftyish and fat, too fat to get into the ring, but he showed us the moves in slow motion. Then we had a small fit soldier who was shifted after a couple of months, and after a few more changes finally we got Murphy. Murphy was a champion and a good one. And he wanted to be welter champ that year. Which is why I found myself in the hall masquerading as a boxer, and a pro at that.

Murphy sparred with all of us in the club but mostly with me. At the time I liked to think it was because I was pretty good, and my greatest moment in the club was when I put him on his arse as he came weaving in. I had already feinted with a left as he did it twice earlier, and the third time I didn't feint. I hit. And Murphy sat down hard. My moment of triumph was brief. He swarmed all over me for the rest of the round, throwing punches from all angles, but somehow I managed to self-defend – nice people used to call boxing self-defence – and I escaped without serious damage to my face and without broken ribs.

It was after that he played the tempter. Walking home from the club talking boxing, night after night, he treated me as an equal, gave me tips and convinced me I was a certainty to be junior champion that year. He was going to be welter champion, he believed. (As it happened he was.) I used to believe him when he said that I would be junior champ, but I never found out if he believed it.

Anyway I was in the frame of mind to be receptive when he asked me to go north with him and box pro under an assumed name. I'd get a fiver for the three rounds, he said, and the fight against a pro would be just what I needed to sharpen me up for the juniors. He'd make sure that my opponent wasn't any great shakes, and he'd be fighting on the same bill: it would be money for oul' rope.

Greed, need, or pride, whatever it was, dictated, and I agreed. That's how I found myself in the pro ring one black-out wartime night. I don't remember anything about the drive in a packed van. There was Murphy and his manager, John, two other boxers with whom I had sparred a few times, and me.

For a few weeks beforehand, I had been stamping my foot and snorting every time I threw a punch. It sounded great, and was, we all thought, real professional. Only one trouble I had with the snorting was that I was inclined to spew snots through my nose when I snorted. Still, I kept at it, and became reasonably competent at snorting without snotting.

There are unmistakable signs about boxers. The edges of their eyebrows are always a little flattened, even if they have never been cut. Although a lot of people believe it, the flattened nose is not necessarily a mark of a boxer. I have known many good ones who never had their noses flattened, and only the bad ones or the unlucky ones got their noses bent or broken. There may or may not be a slight thickening of the ear that's caused by the other guy rubbing either his head or the lace of his glove forcefully along the top of your ear, and it's quite painful, but two certain signs give away a boxer. When he sits, he'll always sit relaxed with his legs apart and his hands joined between them, fingers over fingers and thumb under thumb. That's because he can't join his hands with boxing gloves on them any other way; and when he sits on his little stool in the ring he stretches his legs wide apart to relax them. The most tell-tale of all, though, is the upper lip. It is always slightly thicker than the lower one and over-laps.

For the few weeks before my Big Fight, I shot straight lefts, right crosses and left and right hooks at the mirror in the bedroom, and most of all I cultivated the upper over lower lip position. Why boxers get that way, though with me it was only an affectation, is that you just can't get your lips pressed into that novelist's grim thin line when you're wearing a gumshield. And trying to breathe through your nose – you can't breathe through your mouth with a gumshield stuck between your teeth and the other guy trying to knock them out of your head forces your upper lip out over the lower one. And by the way, the taste of the gutta percha gumshield of the time was bloody awful.

Going into the hall early, I tried to see if my name was on the bill. Murphy's was, or rather his assumed name, in the main event, and I discovered that I was mentioned on the bill alright. I was the other half of the "feather weight preliminary bout featuring Killer McCord". Oh well, I thought, maybe they didn't know my name when they were printing the bill.

It wasn't so bad in the dressing room. Murphy and the other two fighters shared it and we went through the familiar routine: rub down, shadow box, move around, make sheepish jokes, me feeling very naked without a singlet.

But then came the moment of truth and all the dreams faded into stark harsh reality as Murphy and John hustled me down the aisle, half pushed me up the steps, forced me under the ropes, and into the ring. On my own. The others were separated from me by the ropes and for all the help they could give me they might as well have been back in Dublin.

The lights were harsh and exposed everything. They exposed Killer McCord, my opponent, sitting calmly on the stool in the opposite corner, breathing deeply but easily, rippling his muscles with every breath. He had muscles to ripple: I didn't. I must say I don't know exactly what are beetling eyebrows, but whatever they are the Killer had them. He looked tough, rough and mean. He had a few days' bristle on his chin. He had a mat of hair on his chest. His body was deeply tanned.

Shamefacedly I looked down at my own untinted body, gleaming white and juvenile. The green silk shorts which belonged to Murphy flapped forlornly around my thighs. I knew I shouldn't have come. But it was too late to get out now.

Amusement was big business in northern towns in war time where there was plenty of money, as the locals helped the war effort by working overtime, deeming it a more valuable contribution to Britain than donning the uniform and roasting or dying under the desert sun. Professional boxing was an amusement. The halls were packed every week, and the patriotic war workers vicariously vented their blood lust on the Hun by watching the gladiators belt the hell out of each other.

I couldn't bear to look at the Killer any longer, so I turned around and faced into my own corner. Murphy had pale green eyes – cold and ruthless I used to tell myself (in those days I read a lot and was inclined to be a bit romantic). His eyes were boring into me as he plucked what little flesh he could find at the base of my neck near the shoulders.

"Now, I know you're not used to three threes," he was saying, "but it's only three minutes more than you are used to and you're fit. Just keep sticking out your left — that's a good left lead you have — and when you see an opening let fly with a right cross. Keep moving around. Don't let him get in close. Keep the chin well tucked in and your right up to guard. He's a hooker with his left — he doesn't hit straight, so keep going around to his right."

It all went over my head. He was going on: ". . . when I shout last ten just keep throwing punches — catch the referee's eye. Make it look good. This fellow's a ham, he's punchy, you'll take him easy. Carry him for the three rounds." It was a pep talk for a young rawnee, and it failed dismally. I felt miserable. I wasn't frightened, mind you. Not physically scared, because I knew that the Killer wouldn't be let kill me in front of all those people, and I felt from what little experience I had in the ring that I could fairly well keep myself out of trouble, at least for three twos, and I guessed I could stretch that to three threes at a push. I think what I was scared of was that I'd make a fool of myself in front of the crowd. I was always like that.

And then the MC was in the ring, and Murphy whipped the stool from under me, almost before I'd time to stand up. He was wiping my face with a towel, careful not to wipe the eyebrows where the protective but forbidden Vaseline still stood out in thick smears.

"Ladeeze and Gen'lmen," boomed the MC. He wore a dress suit with a black tie, which seemed to my fevered imagination to be gloomily appropriate, and already the perspiration sheened his beefy red face. "Your first contest tonight, on this all-star bill, is the featherweight class between — in the green corner the West Wales champion, KILLER McCORD — " He paused, whether for breath or effect I'll never know, and right on cue, up jumped the Killer, throwing his gloved hands towards heaven, doing a little jig, and waving to the four corners of the hall.

The crowd must have known him. They whistled and shouted and stamped their feet, and there was a claque at the back of the hall whose voices could be heard over the din "Come on, Killer, another kayo! Kill 'im, Killer!" Not at all the kind words I needed to hear in my hour of agony.

Then the MC got in another word edgeways . . . "and in the red corner, the Southern Area champion from Éire, YOUNG KAVANAGH . . ." This blatant lie was received by the crowd with a handful of sympathetic claps, which, after the reception accorded the Killer, echoed around the hall like ghostly bones rattling in a haunted cloister. I glanced around hastily at Murphy, hoping against hope that I was in the wrong place at the wrong time, for I knew my name wasn't Kavanagh, that I wasn't champion of anything, and that so far as the most painstaking research could discover there was no such animal as the Southern Area of Éire in the boxing world. Murphy just shook his head slightly, winked a beady eye and put a sealing finger to his lips.

I was a bit put out over the introduction. I thought my opponent might believe it and with his national pride at stake, come tearing into me like a Welsh Jack Dempsey. He looked capable of it.

Then the referee, a large man in gleaming white, white shin, white tennis trousers and white canvas shoes, had us in the middle of the ring, intoning his ritualistic "I want a clean fight, break when I say break, now shake hands and when the bell goes come out of your corners fighting."

Politely I stuck out my right hand. The Killer, instead of reciprocating, touched my glove lightly with his left and gave me a comradely pat on the chin with his right. To the crowd and the referee it might have looked comradely, but somehow he managed to stick his thumb painfully into the tender gristle of my nose.

Back in the corner, Murphy said "The minute the bell goes, rush out and hit him a one two." So I did. The bell clanged brazenly and I rushed out, met the Killer halfway and let him have a left right to the head. He blinked, snorted and clinched. Somewhat disappointed that he hadn't either gone down flat or had his second throw in the towel, I tried some in-fighting only to find the Killer had my arms tied up in knots while he managed a few short punches to the ribs and the kidney. As well as that he was rubbing his bristly chin on my shoulder – an extraordinarily painful performance. "Break!" shouted the ref and we both backed away, snorting fearfully, gloves weaving in little circles, each of us trying to prove that he hadn't been hurt by the flurry, and that it was only a matter of time before the ref raised our hand in victory.

It's a funny thing, but in the ring the other guy always seems bigger, fitter, more experienced, and more ruthless. Only afterwards do you realise that you were able to hold him, that he was not having it all his own way, that you were able to hurt him, just as he was hurting you, and that he felt exactly the same way about you as you did about him.

The Killer slithered in on the balls of his feet, threw a right cross which I took on my forearm and followed up with a left hook, which fortunately I caught with the point of my elbow hoping viciously that he had broken his wrist through the six-ounce glove. He hadn't; and as I stuck a straight left on his nose, his right came over again and exploded bang on mine. They keep trying to tell you you see stars when you get a hard bang on the head. I never did. What happened was that there was a red flaring ball of an explosion in front of my eyes and the bone of my nose seemed to hit the back of my skull. There was also a warm trickle from my nose down over my upper lip – the one I had cultivated as an overlap all those weeks earlier.

Knowing I was still alive anyway, I dived in desperately to hold on to him as his left hook sizzled past my right ear, the lace of his glove feeling like the prongs of a red-hot fork as it scraped by. But I was inside, with my arms inside his, and he couldn't do me much harm. I tapped gently at his body while he gave me a few pats on the back, the time-honoured tokens of two fighters going though the motions for the ref and the crowd, while taking a breather.

I was snotting blood gently on to his shoulder, and he muttered, "Take it easy, kid. We're not out to kill each other for a few bob. Just make it look good – pull your punches an' I'll pull mine." I had no breath to spare for talk so I made a kind of nodding motion of my head, which smeared more of my blood on the Killer's shoulder, and I hoped he knew that I meant I agreed more than willingly with what seemed to me at that stage his eminently reasonable proposition.

The ref, too, had regard for the proprieties, and he again barked "Break!" reinforcing his order with a slap on the back so we disentangled ourselves and circled warily, feinting and snorting. I was getting into the swing of the thing by now and didn't feel too bad, except that a touch of the oxygen tent would have helped my breathing and my nose felt about six times bigger than normal.

The Killer feinted with his left and I shot over a snappy right cross which caught him just above the eyebrow. In accord with our pact, I had pulled it just at the moment of impact, and it looked good, though it did no damage. The

Killer backed off, nodded his wicked head and gave a slight smile which I took to be approval, then came in with a light left to the body and switched his attack to the head, which it had been expecting, and I slid in under his right to clinch once more. "You're doin' fine," he said, "keep it up." And I felt good. I was proud that a real pro was taking me as his equal until I spotted Svengali Murphy in the corner holding up his ten fingers. That meant, according to instructions, that I should put on a flurry for the "last ten" and I started making like a windmill, tapping Killer's body with light punches, which, I hoped, looked to the fans as if I was giving him a real working-over. Before the inevitable shout of the ref, Killer pushed me away quite gently with his gloves on my shoulder but I saw his on-the-break punch coming and I stepped back out of the way. Before he could follow up, the bell went, and I wheeled smartly and as nonchalantly as I could walked back to my corner.

Murphy had the stool under me, had whipped out my gum shield, and poured a sponge of water over my head letting the wonderful cool fluid flow down my face and neck. He pulled out the elastic of my shorts, handed me the magic bottle to rinse my mouth, pressed the sponge against my nose and was slapping his hands on my calves, all the time keeping up a running fire of talk. "That was a great round, son. You had him on the run there. You're doing well and if you catch with another good right like that, you'll put him away."

Propaganda. Morale boosting stuff, though at the time I took him seriously and felt my chest expand six inches with pride.

A minute is an awful short time in the corner, and I had just begun to relax when that bloody bell went. Murphy whipped the stool away and more or less pushed me out into the lonely centre of the ring again.

The Killer came out briskly, confidently. No touching of gloves this time, just a rapid left hand to the head, which, as I was backing off, didn't hurt, and I shot out a straight left that would have been a beauty had it been a foot nearer its target. He was crowding me, forcing me to give ground, to keep out of range of his punches, even though I knew he was pulling. Strangely enough he kept throwing them, advancing right across the ring and I was taking most of them on my arms when it struck me that if he were really pulling, then his real punches must be fierce.

A snort, a stamp and a looping right screamed over from the Killer but my chin was tucked well in under my left shoulder, as the book said, and it didn't do me any damage, except to numb my left arm down to the elbow. I slithered away easily on the balls of my toes, weaved the magic circle of my fists, as the Killer glared like a bull about to make its final charge in a corrida. This time I waited for him as he came in, head low. My beautiful straight left caught him on the top of his forehead and I thought my wrist was broken; but gallantly again I followed the book and shot over a crisp right cross which caught him high on the temple. He shook his head and dived in to hold on.

Where he got the breath from, I'll never know, yet he said, in a non-gasping voice, "You losing your loaf, kid? Take it easy, same as me." As he said it, he had his bristly chin on my shoulder and was sandpapering my delicate flesh, and his six-ounce gloves were drumming away, though lightly I must admit, at my sparsely fleshed ribs. Recalling an old trick of Murphy's I raised both my arms to show that the Killer was holding on and just as the ref started to bark "Break", the Killer stepped back and slammed a hundredweight of cement into my right side.

There was a satanic grin on his face though he tried to hide it by tucking his chin into his shoulder, and it was then it began to dawn on me that I had been codded.

The Killer wasn't going to take it easy. He hadn't known my strength in the first round, so he wanted time to size me up and he fooled me into going through the motions while he figured out if I was an old pro like himself, or a genuine novice.

It wasn't pleasant to know I had been suckered. It was less pleasant to know that the Killer was an old pro, as experienced in the real thing as my idol Murphy, and for a while I felt panic. He kept coming in at me, shoving lefts and rights which I took mainly on my gloves or on my arms – though a few got through – moving out of his way all the time, giving ground, moving to his right away from that lethal left hook.

In some desperation I stopped retreating and as he was still advancing, feinted with a left, but slipped in a heavy right hook to his ribs. It hurt him. I could see that. But it stopped him only for a second and then he had his arms around me and once more his bristly chin on my shoulder, this time the right one. "So you're being smart, wise guy," he muttered in my reddened ear, "I'll knock the head off you for that." At that stage of the proceedings I was sure he could do just that, and as I hadn't any breath to spare anyway, I didn't answer him, just tried desperately to hit him inside. He was too cute, and I began to think the referee had left the ring, and me to the Killer's vengeance, when I heard that glorious word "break". Believe me, there is no sweeter word in the English language. Yet, I was learning rapidly, and I let the Killer break first. I didn't want another hundredweight of cement in my bruised ribs.

He came at me again with a rush and I did a "pass de sole" of my left foot, bringing my right foot behind sharpish as I did when I was executing a chasse in the ballroom. The Killer swooshed by, arms flailing, so I hit him. Unfortunately for me, he had gone so fast that my punch landed on the back of his head. Which didn't endear me to him, his fans or the referee. That gentleman pushed me away and indicated his very obvious displeasure to the crowd, while warning me that "Once more and you're disqualified."

I nodded, mentally resolving, however, that if the opportunity presented itself again, I'd do the same thing, just to get out of the ring.

"Now box on," snapped the referee, and the Killer was at me again, swarming all over me. I took some of his punches on the gloves, quite a few on the biceps, and a few on the face. I was too busy backing off, covering up and trying to keep out of the way to throw more than a token left, in hope rather than confidence.

At long last, the bell clanged the end of the round, and, head thrown back, I made it to my corner.

I flopped on the stool utterly worn. My nose was so big that I felt each of my eyes was looking around the side of a mountain; my two shoulders were raw; my ribs were on fire and my well-practised overlapping upper lip was torn on the inside. My ear was aflame and my arms hung limply down the sides of the stool.

I'll say this for Murphy. He was a trier. As he and John worked on me, he kept telling me I was going great. I was well ahead on points, only that warning might bring the Killer nearer to me than he should be. (Privately I felt he had been too bloody near all night.) I had him groggy. All I had to do was box him, now, keep him away, just keep sticking out the left, back to his right, and I was a winner. He didn't convince me.

I was nodding my head numbly, trying to appear interested, but in fact, my gaze was fastened on my legs.

I was fascinated by my calf muscles twitching and there was a slight twitch in what passed for my thigh muscles. I didn't feel them twitching and it was none of my volition. Years afterwards I learned that this involuntary twitch was a sure sign of exhaustion, but at the time it didn't matter – I knew I was exhausted anyway. A minute can be a very long time if you're sitting at the telephone hoping your girl will ring. But a minute on the stool in the corner of a ring is like the blinking of an eyelid. With a hissed "Now, dance out and look good," Murphy had flashed the stool away and pushed me out towards my tormentor. The Killer came forward, slithering on the balls of his feet in the text book manner, making the little circles with his gloves and snorting ferociously. I tried to lift my hands to the "Arbour Hill" spar – left hand high, chin tucked into the shoulder and right hand up guarding the head – but somebody had put a pound of lead in each of my six-ounce gloves and the hands would come up only half way. It also took all the effort in the world to get my legs to obey the brain's commands. To me, the Killer looked as fresh as he had before the fight. That's when you begin to lose heart. You know that you've shot your bolt. You're absolutely shagged. And the other guy looks as bright as new paint, apparently ready and able to go another six rounds. It's only an illusion, of course. Your opponent feels the same about you. And it's then the gut stuff takes over. Whichever has the more guts, the more devil in him, the more sheer pig-headed stubbornness not to give in when two fighters are at the end of their tether, will win.

In those days I wasn't given to moralising or analysing sport. Even had I been, it wasn't the place for it, nor was the Killer giving me time. He was in like a flash, left right lancing towards my head, but I swayed back and he was short. Rapidly he switched to the body and landed a short right on my ribs, balancing himself wide to swing the lethal left hook.

Automatically I sent over a looping right, which took him just above his left eye, and as my glove skidded off his temple, the lace brushed him and I was elated to see a thin smear of blood redden his flattened eyebrow. He checked, and I used the respite to circle warily away to his right, still trying to make the appropriate spells in the air with my leaden gloves.

I heard Murphy screaming: "Keep away from him. Box clever. Use the ring." It was admirable advice – if I could have made my legs accept it. They didn't, or at least only in a sluggish tortured fashion that would have shamed a ruptured duck. Again the Killer came forward, aiming a left hook high at my head. I forced my right hand to block it, then stuck out a left which he brushed aside, nearly knocking me off balance.

We were in the middle of the ring sparring, feinting, looking for an opening and McCord flung himself at me, getting inside, drumming his gloves on my body, while I shoved my elbows tight into my ribs, to absorb his punches.

Then the nightmare took over. Time had no meaning. I was no longer fully conscious. My hands and legs obeyed my brain hours later. My mouth was dry. My gum shield flew out and I thought: "Oh, God, there's a mouthful of teeth gone." Still there was no rush of blood down my throat, nor was there any pain, so I just kept doggedly on. When the Killer backed, I stumbled forward, trying to send out punches, trying to get in close to hang on. He moved backwards, counter-punching, yet though he landed frequently, he didn't hurt.

My whole being was in agony. From the chest down, there was just a hollow inside me, and I felt that I must puke or die. My arms and legs didn't seem to belong to me any more. My forehead was sore, my eyes felt as if they were closed, and the only conscious thought in my mind was "Oh, God, will it ever be over?"

The Killer jabbed a straight right which landed on the side of my face, and he fell in behind it, head landing on my shoulder, gloves resting on my biceps and we wrestled around, neither of us able to do more. I was vaguely flapping my gloves in the direction of his tanned body, content to stay that way with him forever, so long as they didn't ask me to move again. It was never going to end and I didn't care any longer. The lights, the crowd, the referee, Murphy, John, the whole lot had gone. There was only me and the Killer locked together. Forever, as it seemed.

An eternity later, I heard someone say "Break, it's over," and that didn't mean anything, until white-clad arms came between the Killer and me and forced us apart. Somehow, I was in my own corner, and Murphy slammed the sponge on the top of my head, and turned me around to push me into the centre of the ring again.

This time, there was no enemy to face. Instead, the referee took my arm and stood between me and Killer McCord, whose arm he held in his left hand. The MC, still in his funereal suit, nearly split my ear with the bellow: "Ladeeze and gen'lmen, the winner of that featherweight contest – KILLER McCORD."

Now I could hear the whistles and the stamps and the cheers and the claps. The Killer, who so recently had been trying to take my head off the shoulders, leaped in the air, waving his two gloves aloft, then came at me and hugged me, patting the back of my head affectionately, murmuring something encouraging, and walked me back to my own corner. For which bit of chivalry he got an extra cheer.

It's an extraordinary thing that when two fighters have met and fought as hard as they can in the ring, there grows a peculiar bond of affection between them. Whether you've thumped him into a pulp or he has beaten you hollow, there is a sort of love for your opponent that endures long after you've both retired from boxing. I never met Killer McCord again, in the ring or out of it, so I still remember him with a sort of affection.

The borrowed dressing gown was slung around my shoulders, a towel wrapped Arab fashion over my head, and John shepherded me up the aisle to the dressing rooms.

I lay on the table as somebody started to massage my cruelly over-exerted limbs, and my belaboured ribs. Now I could feel the dull ache in my swollen nose, the rawness of my shoulders, the soreness of my ribs, the ineffable weariness of my whole body.

Paddy, one of the other boxers, was shuffling around the room shadow-boxing. Through his forcibly expelled breathing he was telling me I did well, I had him licked until I ran out of steam, I'd have to train for three threes and I'd murder him in the return. I was becoming a cynic by now, and once more I didn't believe what I was being told. It was enough just to lie there, an ice bag giving blessed relief to my nose which didn't altogether block my view now.

I was still in the dressing room when Paddy was carried back. He'd been kayoed in the first minute. The other boxer walked back. He'd won and he was talking nineteen to the dozen to John, re-living the fight, every single blow and parry of it.

Showered and dressed, pleasantly tired and with some stiffness in different parts of my anatomy, I joined the others at the ringside to watch Murphy win the main bout of the evening after a hard and good fight.

Later, after the lights in the hall were out and nothing remained of the action except the smell of tobacco smoke and sweat and embrocation, we walked through the blacked-out streets to the van, eating chips from paper bags. The winners and John were in high spirits, and the resilient Paddy – I think he was a bit punchy – was already making plans for his next fight. But I was silent. Every time I put a chip in my mouth the salt and vinegar stung the cut inside my upper lip. I had my fiver. I hadn't disgraced myself. But I knew in my heart I wasn't going to win the juniors that year. Or any other year. I had retired.

Chapter 6

The Sporting Life (2)

Alone amongst a sea of Leeds United and Manchester United shoulder bags floated one lonely West Ham duffle, as about forty kids milled around the gate of Stella's ground. It was the day of the trials for the under-11s and it was now 2.45. The trials were scheduled for three o'clock, but since half one, they had begun to arrive – in twos and threes, in groups of five and six – even a couple of them came solo.

They were of all sizes and shapes, though the West Ham supporter, a big soft and soft-faced kid, stood head and shoulders over the others. The shrill babble of voices sounded like the twittering of a million insects on that late August afternoon, and the gods were invoked – Giles, Lorrimer, Best, Charlton. On their faces you could see hope, confidence and doubt all blending. In their eyes were the visions of glory, and already every one of them saw himself the star at Wembley four or five years hence.

A lad of about eighteen pushed his way through the mob, and you could see from the way he had the key to the gate that he was the manager. The crowd sensed it, and swarmed around him like bees around the queen, every one of them trying to attract his attention, tugging at his clothes, calling

"Mister, mister, I play in the back four." "Mister, I'm a striker." "Mister, I'm a midfielder" . . . but he patiently alrighted them and pushed open the gate. They surged through, yelping and jostling, afraid that the last few in wouldn't get a trial with Stella Maris.

The manager blew a sharp blast on a whistle and shouted at them to line up in two lines. "Everyone will get a trial," he told them, "but first I have to get your names and your positions. If you don't line up and stay quiet, I'll call off the trial." They couldn't stay quiet, they were too excited for that, but the threat at least had the effect of reducing them to some sort of order, and the manager went along, taking names, asking "What position do you play?" They told him, some of them with great aplomb, others telling him they played anywhere, still others urging: "Won't you find that out, sir?" At the back of their eyes you could see the fear that the admission might cause them to be sidelined, but withal, their simplicity wouldn't let them tell the lie direct.

It was well after half-three before the first twenty-two were lined up in some semblance of two football teams on the bright sunlit pitch and the others, impatient, and unable to contain themselves, twitched and walked and ran and danced up and down the sidelines. They didn't want to watch. They wanted to be out there in the thick of it, proving themselves to the manager.

With a sharp blast of his whistle the young fellow set them off and very professionally the centre-forward tipped the ball to his inside man. Like two packs of hounds in full cry after a sighted fox, the twenty of them chased the ball, shrill halloos rising every time it broke from the crowd, and they streamed away, first one way, then the other, panting, eager, kicking, pushing, all impressing, as they thought, the manager.

With the yelps of "Here, fella", and "Right, Tom", they ranged the four corners of the field, young faces tight with tension, young skinny legs flashing in the gaily coloured stockings. This wasn't Stella Maris ground in Richmond Road. This was Wembley, Aztec Stadium, Dalymount, all the famous grounds in the world rolled into one, and now, no longer were they playing in a trial. In their little minds they were already the Bests, the Charltons, the Peles.

Half an hour was enough. There was another batch to be tried and to the blast of the whistle the acolytes reluctantly trooped off, their field taken by the impatient remainder.

Again the manager sorted the confusion, and again the whistle signalled the start of the chase. Different boys, twenty-two of them, but the same. Again the dream world had taken over for the newcomers, and again fervidly they chased that ball all over Stella's well-tended pitch. One or two in each trial had natural skill. Others showed that they could have potential. All of them had enthusiasm and hope.

The manager ran around with the pack, trying, mostly vainly, to give some kind of instruction. But they were young, intent on the chase like over-eager hounds closing for the kill: their eyes and ears and minds were closed to anything but the pursuit of the ball.

As usual, I was on the sidelines, an observer and bystander. I envied the manager his youth, his patience and his dedication.

The long shrilling of the whistle proclaimed the end of the session and the unsatisfied footballers were herded to the dressing rooms for a shower and commanded to "line up outside in two rows". The showers were perfunctory. Who'd waste time on a wash when the big moment was at hand? In a matter of minutes, they knew, they all knew, they were going to be signed, and they were on the road to stardom.

The manager walked down the two lines "you ... and you ... and you. . . come back for a trial on Tuesday at half-six."

Eighteen times, he said "you" and eighteen faces lit up, skinny shoulders squared with a new arrogance. Eighteen under-11s clamoured around him, asking endless questions, wanting to know when did the league start, how much training did they do, when was the first match?

But more than eighteen heads drooped, slim shoulders slumped. Even the duffle bags seemed dejected as the rejected slunk out through the gate. West Ham was amongst them, and the poor kid's eyes glistened with tears which he fought to hold back as alone he shuffled away from Stella's ground.

I stood on the wings, as usual. The manager looked at me with a mute appeal in his eyes. They were saying, "What could I do? There's only one pitch. There are so few of us to give the time to the kids. There'll be only one team. Even from the eighteen, more kids are going to be disappointed." Then, desperately, the eyes said to me, "Why doesn't the bloody government or the corporation or the schools or somebody provide facilities for the kids?"

I turned away from the appeal. Like himself, I could do nothing for the disappointed kids, only weep in my soul that any child had to be hurt because somebody up there didn't care about the kids while they wasted our money on their own pride and for their own ends.

Chapter 7

People I Never Met

Two people who impinged on my life and exerted a considerable influence on it, though I never had the pleasure of meeting them, were Anon and A.N. Other. They were ubiquitous in the spheres of most interest to me, sport and writing, in my uneventful journey through this vale of tears.

A.N. Other was an all round sportsman, equally proficient at cricket, football, hurling, hockey, indeed any team game.

He first crossed my path many years ago when I was playing for Home Farm as a kid. At the time, the now defunct *Evening Mail* was essential reading on Fridays, for that admirable publication carried notice of all the team selections for the Sunday matches ("Meet at McBirney's 11 a.m. sharp"). On Friday after Friday during the season I fidgetted and fretted for what seemed hours until my father had finished his ritual reading of the *Mail*, and I could grab it to see if my name figured in the team list for Dermy Flanagan's under fourteens.

For a long time that season, A.N. Other was an automatic choice at left full-back, the position I felt should be mine by right of zealous training and ineffable longing, if not by outstanding merit, but Kelly was usually the first reserve. There weren't panels or subs in those days and the reserve got his place only if there was a last-minute defection from the selected team.

I was always at McBirney's at a quarter to eleven, for "11 a.m. sharp" on those Sundays, having said a guilty prayer or two earlier at Mass that somebody wouldn't turn up, not praying that any serious harm would come to him, just that he'd be late or have a toothache or a cold or a sprained ankle or something mild like that.

Eagerly scanning the faces of the other players milling around with their stockings stuffed into their boots and their boots stuffed under their arms, I dreaded the moment when I'd see an unfamiliar face, because that would surely be the manly handsome visage of A.N. Other. Idly, I wondered why he deserved two initials while the rest of us merited only surnames, and I suffered from a chronic grievance that this fellow Other never turned up for training.

Yet he was picked before me who trained himself into exhaustion, and Dermy had a strict rule that if you didn't train, you didn't play. No matter who you were. Even Jackie Carey, who was the star of the big fellows' team, the Minors, wouldn't get his place if he didn't turn up for training, unless he had a legitimate excuse, such as a broken leg.

Heaven was nearer on those Sundays in the icy windswept Fifteen Acres when Dermy threw me a blue and white hooped jersey – nobody wore football "shirts" then – with the curt instruction "Strip, Kelly, you're playing." Omar under his bough with his jug and his thou couldn't have been happier than I under the bare goalpost with my jersey and my boots, and quick as a flash I was out of my clothes and into my costume to masquerade as a footballer, knowing that Dermy, hard taskmaster though he was, wouldn't be so hard-hearted as to take the jersey from me once I had donned it.

Also, I was determined that if by any chance he tried, he'd have to have me held down by the rest of the team and forcibly denuded.

Hastily intoning a mental Te Deum, followed by an Act of Contrition for praying ill on my unknown team mate, I was always first on the field, sprinting up and down in the corner farthest from the non-existent pavilion, just out of hailing distance, until the teams lined out.

It wasn't until a few years afterwards that someone explained to me that A.N. Other was just another way of writing "another", meaning that the manager hadn't chosen to fill the position until just before the match, and it gave me a sort of let-down, just as Finian must have had when he came to the end of his rainbow and found there was no crock of gold. To me, for all that time A.N. was a real person, a superstar who could play anywhere in any game, and though I half-hated him for his superior ability, perversely, I wanted to meet him.

The other fellow Anon, was in a different line of business, though equally as versatile and as brilliant as A.N. Other. He was a writer, philosopher and poet. He was multilingual. Equally at home in Irish, English, Latin, Greek and French, he was a prolific writer on many diverse subjects. It was in the *Golden Treasury of Verse* I first made his acquaintance, when his by-line appeared under many lovely pieces in that excellent introduction to poetry. And, just to show no coolness, he turned his hand to Irish poetry, contributing generously of his talents to the classic collection, *Fíon na Filíochta*. Unless my memory is faulty, it was he who wrote "Ag Críost an Síol", that lovely old Irish prayer, and to demonstrate his versatility, he also supplied a lullaby "Do Chuirfinn-se Féin mo Leanbh a Chodladh". His nature poem "Crónán na mBeach", is ranked in the "*Fíon*" with some offerings by Oisín, the son of Fionn Mac Cumhaill who presumably wrote them some time before he slipped off his white horse on a return visit to the Emerald Isle. He didn't make it back to Tír na nÓg that time.

Treatises, homilies, reports of battles: it was all the one to our friend. Anon was in there pitching with the best of them, out-writing even the top boys, Julius, Xenophon, Shakespeare and Wilde. I bet he wrote more than any of them. And he didn't confine himself to any one age, or any one line of business. He dispensed gems of wisdom, pointed parables and picturesque phrases bountifully. The *Reader's Digest* relied heavily on his homespun philosophy, and I was one of his most devoted readers.

I must have been very naïve, even silly, for it took me years to realise that Anon at the end of a piece didn't mean "soon", in the sense that his name would be revealed in subsequent issues, but that it really meant the publisher had no idea who had written the thing.

I really wanted to know his identity so I could say or write to him: "That was a grand bit of poetry you wrote," or "that bit of advice you gave was priceless." Not like the people to whom I'm "Anon" today and on whose circumstances I've exerted some influence.

There are those whom I have helped into jobs in the highest rank of the public service, Dáil Éireann. Religiously over the past thirty years or so, at their behest, I have trotted out my franchise for a bit of exercise and sent a messenger or two to the Dail to represent me. You'd think they'd try to find out, even occasionally, who I am, or how I feel about their stewardship, or if I wanted a bill or two introduced up there in the Dail. Not on your life. Not one of them has walked up the short avenue where I have my abode for so long as I can pay the mortgage, to find out anything about me.

To the barmen whom I've kept in jobs over a long time, I'm nothing but a "Hello . . . Eh." To the bookies, brewers, cigarette makers, and distillers I'm only a dot on the profit side of their balance sheets. To my ground landlord, though I've helped make him a bloated capitalist, I'm only a letter box into which he can send demands. To my longest-standing pen pal, my Income Tax Inspector, I'm a mere number, though if I weren't on his books, his overtime would be severely curtailed.

I see Paddy McGrath at a lot of race meetings and he looks through me, as if I didn't exist. Where would he be, I wonder if I didn't buy a ticket for every one of his sweeps?

The more I think of it, the more annoyed I become at being Anon. No Taoiseach has ever known me, which is a pity, for he could have dropped into Barney's or the Inn any Friday night about ten o'clock and got the solution to his country's problems, though conversely the only reason I'd want a Taoiseach to know me would be so he could make me a senator.

President Reagan of the U.S.A., I'm sure, isn't like the rest of them. I bet every time he takes his finger off the button or puts down the hot-line telephone to Russia and his feet on the desk in the Oval Office, he's saying to himself, "I still remember that Anon who shook hands with me after the Catholic Stage Guild Concert in the Adelphi in Dublin in 1948." Ronnie, as I called him then, is a simple man I'm sure, as simple as I was when I puzzled over the identities of A.N. Other and Anon.

My erstwhile favourite author, Anon, was and is a humorist, amongst his many other attributes, and one of my favourites in that sphere is his story of the lady in Galway who visited her husband in the death cell on the night before he was to be hanged. He had probably committed some heinous crime like refusing to sell his horse to a Protestant for a fiver or stealing food for his children, for it was in the Penal Days that he met his doom.

His wife waffled on for some considerable time, about the neighbours, the children, the weather, and country gossip. At last she paused for breath, and noticed her spouse didn't seem to be listening to her with rapt attention.

"What's wrong with you at all tonight?" she asked. "Is it huffy you are because you're being hanged in the morning?"

Chapter 8

Creative Writing

Thanks to Miss Sharpe in Gardiner Street Convent School, I was able to read at an early age, and of all the headlines I remember reading away back in the dim past was one in the *Evening Herald* proclaiming the scandal of "Mixed Bathing in Portmarnock". It must have been an awful long time ago, for in the mid-thirties I was frolicking in the same waters, and there were young ladies a-plenty in our company. Another headline I recall is one which appeared in the *Sunday People*, announcing the death of Lawrence of Arabia, who, under the alias of A/C Shaw of the British Royal Air Force, had died in a motor-cycle accident. I had no idea then how newspapers were produced, nor who produced them, nor that men were employed in newspaper offices. I hadn't the curiosity to think about them at all except as something to read, and later on, to check if I were listed to attend "Ballast Office 11 a.m".

There are unkind people who will say I still have no idea how newspapers are produced. They will be mostly the younger lot, for there are very few remaining who remember that for one glorious period, albeit short, I was EDITOR of a daily newspaper.

It was in 1952 and I was working for Harpers, Martin

Francis Coffey's publishing company. He produced a number of periodicals, annuals, church year-books, monthly magazines and even guidebooks. I was more or less his main writer, and as well as covering the ballrooms under the name of Tango, I was Industrial Correspondent, hagiographer, advertising copy-writer, personality interviewer, and editor for some of his magazines. He paid the union rate, a guinea and a half per thousand words for periodicals; the newspaper rate for features was two guineas an article. Martin was a grand man to work for, kind and considerate, and he paid on acceptance. That is, even if a publication wasn't scheduled to appear until perhaps, three months later, he paid as soon as he had accepted the copy.

More than once, he paid an impecunious journalist in advance of receiving copy, and more than once he never did receive it, but that didn't sour him, and he was always ready to give a hand to someone who was out of work temporarily, or use the influence of his personality to fix him up with a job. It was, in fact, Martin's firm which paid for my first car, a Y-model Ford, which cost me £50 or 34 articles for Harpers. It was Martin who made me editor of the *News Record*.

For some months in 1952, there had been the threat of a strike by Dublin printers, members of the D.T.P.S., and a few people had been considering running a daily if the strike, which would close all the Dublin papers, came off. I was only half aware of all the negotiations and failing talks, because I was working my head off, and as usual minding my own business, which, on July 11, involved an evening at *Faust*. Opera was never my passion, as I could never restrain my sense of the ridiculous when watching an eighteen-stone male singer bellowing tender love into the ear of a fourteen-stone soprano, and she screaming back at him, all this going on in some foreign language to a tremendous din from the orchestra. I must have made a serious error of judgement in my most recent female companion, for she it was who wanted to see *Faust,* and the affaire lasted until I had escorted her home after the performance.

After I'd left her, I made my way home, and like the dog at his father's wake, I was neither glad nor sorry I wouldn't be seeing her again. It was just as well I'd made no romantic plans for the immediate future, as a telegram awaited me: "Get down to Dakota right away. Get Taxi. Martin." I guessed it was important, if he was paying for a taxi, so I did as I was bid, as they say in Dublin, to find Dakota in a state of organised chaos. When Martin Coffey's face was flushed, he was flustered, and it was flushed when I came into the office. Busy sub-editing a pile of copy, he flung most of it at me, telling me to get busy. I was the editor, and he was going to be managing editor, available for consultation, but not expected to get into the slog. He'd the publishing firm to run during the day, and he was an older man than I.

In snatches I heard the story. The operation had been set up for a couple of weeks, and was ready to swing into action as soon as the strike came off. It wasn't a scab paper, because arrangements had been made with the D.T.P.S. to supply printers, who would be paid the full amount demanded of the Dublin papers. Later in the week, when we needed more Linotype operators, I had to contact the union, and it was either Liam McGrath or Martin McGrath who looked after the supply of staff to us; I learned that the union was quite glad to have its members working instead of drawing strike pay, and further, it considered the production of a daily paper would force the established newspapers to settle the strike. There were a number of people buzzing around that first night, but the only one I clearly remember on the editorial side, besides Martin Coffey and myself, was Arthur, whom I detailed to do the stone. A stone subeditor works on a table called the stone with a compositor, laying out the pages of type, which are cast in lines of lead. It is an important job, as the stone sub is responsible for the layout of the pages.

In the meantime I listened to the news bulletins on the radio, took the news down in shorthand, sub-edited and sent it out for setting. At half-two in the morning all the copy was out with the printers and I went to the caseroom to see how many pages had been laid out. It was vital that we get all the copy set by the lino men and the pages made up on the stone very early, because the printing machine we had was capable only of printing 1,200 copies an hour; since we had to be on the streets by half-seven in the morning, we should have to start printing before midnight to make our target of 20,000 copies.

Arthur, many years my senior, and many years in journalism, had a weakness for the drink. Perhaps I wrong him, for his weakness was probably only a little stronger than most, yet when I found him slumped snoring on the stone, I was displeased. Yanking him awake I put him in a taxi and sent him home, at the expense of the firm, with a vicious warning not to come back unless he was going to remain sober.

Then I had to get stuck into the stone myself, and it was five o'clock in the morning before we started printing. As it happened it didn't make much difference because the newspaper-starved citizens of the metropolis bought the *Record* even on their way home from work. Arthur's fall was indirectly the fault of Martin Coffey, the managing editor. A good organiser, and always mindful of the needs of a journalist, Martin had granted a local public house a personal exemption order, and by giving a secret knock at the side door, the staff of the *News Record* could have access for refreshment up to about 3 a.m.. Some of the market's pubs opened at five in the morning which was convenient, as work could be done in the intervening two hours.

After a couple of days, we got more organised and took on some journalists, freelances who were unemployed because of the strike. The staff men, who were not on strike, were still reporting for duty to their papers and being paid. Wild horses wouldn't drag the names from me of a couple who brought us carbon copies of some foreign news, and of course, we lifted from the radio bulletins. Mick Dwyer, God rest him, did the courts, and the late Eric O'Leary, the lovable racing writer, looked after racing. Des Murphy was a barman in Humphreys in Moore Street and was a first-class barman, but being an intelligent man, he wanted more out of life. As he was au fait with GAA affairs, I appointed him our GAA correspondent, and after the strike had ended he decided to try his hand at freelance journalism. I gave him an introduction to Seamus Devlin of the *Irish Press,* and Des never looked back.

There was a two-day or three-day race meeting in Tramore, and I detailed Eric to cover it for us, naturally paying his expenses and salary to which he was entitled. The first evening of the meeting he came on the phone to give us his report and results, and as I was taking the copy, I remarked to him it was a very clear line.

A couple of minutes later, I heard the five-minutes pips and Eric begging somebody for coppers to put in the phone! Sensible man that he was, Eric had arranged with a colleague to give him the results, saving himself a journey to Tramore: he was telephoning his report from our local friendly and accommodating pub.

We were all being paid above the rate and the promoters were making a lot of money, especially since the advertisers were fighting each other to buy space in our paper, there being no other, but it was hectic and very tiring, and between one thing and another, I found myself working nearly sixteen hours a day. I think the only thing that kept me going for the few months was that I met Padraig O'Raghallaigh, the Radio Éireann announcer, each evening at half-five and we went swimming before returning to his house for a meal. Padraig was studying for his MA at the time and was working as many hours as I was. About the middle of August, his wife Peg more or less ordered us to take a holiday, and off we went to Ernie Evans' Towers Hotel in Glenbeigh for a week. We swam and we drank and we talked and joined sing-songs and we relaxed; We went to Puck Fair, the only time I ever saw it, and stepped over fighting tinkers on the floor of the pub to order our pints and generally enjoyed the manifestations of our national heritage.

I'd been trying to save a few pounds to buy a car and I came home broke to find there'd been a bloodless coup in the *Record,* and I had been ousted. I suppose it just shows you should never take holidays if you want to keep your job. The strike ended a couple of weeks later, and the *News Record* joined the *Skibbereen Eagle, Freeman's Journal, The Nation* and many other illustrious newspapers, in oblivion. I didn't care. Sometimes, however, I wonder if any copy of it has survived the years.

There are no Communists in Ireland now: they're all Socialists, or Marxists, or Leninists or Trotskyites or anti-Nationalists, or Left Wingers, and they all believe in Democracy. The Communists were officially declared non-existent as far back as 1953. I know, because I had a part in the declaration.

I was working as a reporter for an editor who was very pro-Nationalist. He might even be called patriotic, if that weren't a hideous insult nowadays, and he was perturbed at the growth of communism in Dublin. He detailed me to do an investigation and I spent three weeks working on the assignment, the results of which proved that the Communist Party, and some other fellow-travelling organisations were gradually expanding their membership. At that time, communists didn't openly proclaim themselves as Marxist-Leninists and though the Communist Party was in existence, it had no mass appeal. I handed the story to my editor, who was very pleased with my efforts, complimented me and said it would appear on the following week. It didn't. Nor did it appear the week after that. The editor apologetically called me into his office eventually to let me know the report wasn't going to appear. "The story was first-class," he told me. "It won't be going into the paper, however, because the powers that be won't let it. Apparently, Communism, or Fascism couldn't flourish under our government." I had no great feeling one way or the other, though having no great ambition to become a Stakhanovite, the news was vaguely comforting.

One of my great friends in those days was the late Tom Burns, a young Belfastman who came to Dublin, having worked on the *Belfast Telegraph*. He was taken on as a temporary reporter in the newsroom of Radio Éireann, where he showed his competence over six months. Poor Tom, he was destined to suffer the same experience as I did, for a vacancy for a reporter arose and was advertised. As he'd been doing the job well for six months, I regarded him as a certainty, but when he was asked at the interview if he had any Irish, he had to admit that, as he was educated in the North, he hadn't had any opportunity to learn it; therefore, he didn't get the job. So, not having time to learn the Gaelic, Tom had to set about keeping the wolf from the door *sans* the miraculous amulet of the native tongue.

Anyhow, at my request, Martin Coffey saw that Tom Burns didn't starve by engaging him to write for his publications, and Tom was also picking up a few days, casual work in the *Irish Times.* I asked Douglas Gageby, then assistant editor of the *Sunday Press,* to hire Burns on Saturdays, as that paper required additional staff on Saturdays. Douglas, now boss of the *Irish Times,* did and very soon afterwards, Tom was put on the staff, and eventually became news editor. He was the only man I ever knew who stopped the presses.

Long ago, "Stop Press" editions used come out on very rare occasions. Stopping the presses means holding up the production run, to change the front page. It can be a costly exercise for any newspaper, and a Stop Press for anything but a really big story is a short-cut to the dole queue.

Tom was alone in the newsroom in the *Sunday Press* in the early hours of the morning, and was making the last routine telephone check when a telephone operator told him casually there'd been a murder in Co. Kildare. Tom chased the story, which was the murder of a girl named Curran, coincidentally the name of a girl in the North who'd been murdered a few weeks earlier. He stopped the presses and ran the story on the front page, and it was exclusive to the *Sunday Press.*

He won that one, though he told me he sweated blood until the Tuesday conference confirmed his judgement. He could have cost the paper thousands of pounds if he'd made the wrong decision.

I made a wrong decision one night in Radio Éireann, and it may have been that which cost me the job there. Unfortunately I was right, but I was right to the wrong man, which is as bad as being wrong to any man. Some cardinal was visiting the country and I went to the B & I ship on which he travelled, to interview him. It was a purely routine effort. He wasn't another Saint Patrick nor was he a Father Lefebvre. He was just a cardinal on a private visit, and the only tricky thing about it was the protocol.

You see, while it doesn't matter a fiddler's to the hundreds of thousands of readers or listeners, the order in which very important people are mentioned matters an awful lot to the VIPs. It's called Protocol, or in Americanese, Pecking Order, and people who get into the Order are very tetchy about it. My cardinal was on a private visit and after getting a few platitudes from him for my report, I sought out his secretary to clarify the pecking order. Following his advice, I listed the cardinal after the President. That's how it went out on the 10.15 p.m. bulletin. Forty-five minutes later, when I was alone in the newsroom, I had a visit from the civil servant who was in charge of administration in the radio station. Radio Éireann was owned by the civil servants then. I don't know who owns it now, but it's certainly not the public, the people who pay for it.

Without putting a tooth in it, this man wanted me to change the report, putting the cardinal as head man in the list. The Secretary, he said, and you could almost hear the capital letters, suggested the change. I told him I'd already checked with the fons et origo, the cardinal's sec., and refused. He persisted and I resisted, and that was the end of the matter so far as I was concerned. Later, however, after I'd got the job that I didn't get eventually, and Michael Lawlor told me the "civil servants wouldn't have me", that incident did cross my mind. I didn't blame the cardinal nor the Church, and I certainly didn't think the Church in toto was to blame for a period of fast imposed on John Ross and me one raw November night.

Another Church dignitary, it may have been a nuncio, I'm not sure, was due to arrive at Dublin Airport at about three in the afternoon, and we were to interview him. The news was quite innocuous and innocent in those far-off days, no armed robberies, no Gardaí murdered. We had to make do with politicians and clergymen and reports of the Haganah and the Stem Gang in Palestine, and of course, the Dáil. Luckily for television, times have changed and they get plenty of pictures of blood and violence for the newscasts.

We waited. In the open, in the freezing cold, we waited for three hours because the plane was late. At last the Excellency – I'm pretty certain he was an Excellency – landed, but he was hustled into his car and dashed over to the Nunciature in the Park. John and I played cops and robbers after him and reached it a few minutes after he did. Once more we were foiled. A flunkey told us His Excellency was having his dinner, but we could wait inside the door, and we did, starving, and sniffing enticing food smells for another hour. At last the VIP came in, hand extended. John stuck his out and shook hands, I made the proper obeisance, and we got a few words of an interview. John was not of the Faith, but he quoted something which sounded biblical about feeding the hungry as we made our starved way back to Henry Street.

John was one of the best broadcasters radio ever had. Quiet and unflappable, he had a radio style equalled by few. He was also part of what afterwards was known as the Bohemian Set, to which he introduced me, and there was a constant stream of people, including Ernie Gebler, who "discovered" Edna O'Brien (and also wrote a book about the Plymouth Brethren which was made into a film starring Spencer Tracy), George

Morrison, who made *Mise Éire* and *Saoirse*, and Hoddie, dropping into R.É. to chat with him. Hoddie was, and presumably still is, George Hodnett, who is a jazz expert and is noted for the stub of a cigarette which always hangs from his upper lip. He scared the hell out of me one night.

John Ross lived with his family in Woodtown, a house which once belonged to Eoin MacNeill, out past Rathfamham, and it was a rural liberty hall. All kinds of people dropped in and stayed with them, sometimes for months: actors resting, artists unemployed and creative people who had not created anything, either profitable or unprofitable, though they were always going to.

I was visiting John in Woodtown when Hoddie arrived by car. I don't think his sight was too good for he wore very thick glasses and yet, as it was raining when he offered me a lift home, I was glad to accept. It really rained, the strong wind blowing it into the car, which I think was a Morris, without a windscreen. Hoddie had the remedy. He simply fastened an old army groundsheet in place of the windscreen, and peering out through a small opening in the groundsheet, drove down the hilly darkening roads like the clappers. I couldn't see out and just in case I might, I kept my eyes tightly closed as Hoddie hummed a tune to himself driving nonchalantly as far as Baggot Street where he dropped me, alive, much to my surprise. I never travelled with him since then.

I can't vouch for this story as I wasn't directly involved, but I did meet the Bohemians the night after it was alleged to have happened and it was the subject of the conversation: There was an artist who was part of the set, and he coveted what is now called in the media the live-in girlfriend of a fringe member, his mistress, in fact, with whom the fringe member lived in a small cottage in the mountains. Influenced by passion and alcohol, the artist decided the only way he could have the woman was by shooting the man in possession, and he had an accomplice, another nut, drive him to the spot. They lay in the gorse all night, the lover with a loaded shotgun, waiting for the first light when the live-in lover was to be blasted. He wasn't.

The tale told by the "gunman" when they finally returned stiff with the cold, and hungry, to what passed for civilisation in those circles, was that he was fully determined to do the deed, but when the man came through the door in the morning, scratching himself as everyone does on getting up, and yawning, before urinating in the open, the scene was of such touching domesticity that he couldn't bring himself to spoil it by pulling the trigger. It sounds crazy, but they were, and I believe the story.

None of the set seemed to have a full-time job, or regular source of income, though they managed to live quite well. Of course it has to be remembered they were young and probably symbolic of the non-conformity of the young, which has manifested itself in the intervening decades in more repulsive forms. There were the parties in the Catacombs, yet, looking back on them, these were only following in the old tradition of Dublin hooleys, if perhaps a little more uninhibited. Most of them who survived are now middle-aged conformists, having established themselves in their chosen fields. Mick Dunleavy didn't do too badly, nor Ernie Gebler, nor George Morrison. Neither, in fact, did John Ross, who has resumed thriller writing in addition to his other activities.

It was John who influenced me to try my luck at writing features, something I had never done earlier, and success attended my first effort. I wrote a feature and sent it to the *Herald*. It was published a few days later, and I knew then I was better than George Bernard Shaw, who tried for six years before he was paid by a publisher. Two guineas the *Herald* paid me for "Television is Sweeping the World", which encouraged me to write another for that excellent publication. This time, I had to wait for two weeks before it appeared, and since then, I have written millions of words, and received enough rejection slips to paper a room. John also introduced me to Liam MacGabhann of the *Sunday Press,* and that led to my association with the paper which has lasted since the early days of that organ.

I covered the press conference announcing the Tóstal, that peculiar concept of a countrywide boost to Tourism, which led to all kinds of social activities designed to bring tourists, not alone from one part of the country to another but also from foreign parts.

The official carnival opening of An Tóstal was set for a Sunday. For months beforehand, O'Connell Bridge housed a wooden structure guarded like Fort Knox, and containing the Bowl of Light, the motif of An Tóstal. Flower beds were set up behind the masking structure and the Bowl was to be lit by some Terribly Important Person to declare open the festival. Nobody was allowed to look inside the barriers.

About one o'clock on that Sunday morning, I was finishing a work shift, and Terry O'Sullivan, the eminent columnist called me into his office to have a drink. Then he had the idea we should have a run up town, to see if anything was happening, and off we went in his car. From Burgh Quay we could see the crowds gathering on the bridge and by the time we got to the Bridge, the crowd had gone berserk. The wooden structure was torn down. The Thing, as Dubliners who weren't in on the secret called the Bowl of Light, was flung into the Liffey. Now absolutely rabid, the mob tore up

O'Connell Street, smashing shop windows, overturning cars and creating mayhem in the loveliest thoroughfare in Dublin that was. What had happened to change a good-humoured late night Dublin crowd into a pillaging mob, I never found out.

Our car was lucky. We crawled through the mob, turned around the Parnell Monument, parked the car at the back and went into the Gresham Hotel, where Toddy O'Sullivan entertained us for an hour or so. That end of O'Connell Street was almost unscathed. The rest was like a battlefield. It was, I suppose, a striking opening to the festival which lingered on for some years before gently expiring.

The island is still there on O'Connell Bridge. The flower beds are long gone, and The Thing was recovered from the river many years later.

Many journalists are inclined to forget the responsibility they bear, most likely because they are doing the same job every day, and some of them, not too many, think that because they are journalists they are somehow superior to other beings, especially readers. I have to admit that for some time, I felt a bit like that. The *Sunday Press* was giving me big publicity for my football articles and literally all over the country for a couple of years they had my picture on posters, outside, it seemed, nearly every newspaper shop. I was feeling a bit smug one day driving home from a match in Sligo, not exactly counting the posters, but appreciating them. As I passed one in a village outside Longford, a little dog came up, lifted his leg, and urinated on "Big Bill". That sic transitted my bit of gloria, forever.

When I went to Radio Éireann first as an "assistant" in the newsroom, the news service was being brought into the twentieth century: a staff was appointed; teleprinters to carry the news from the agencies were installed; and a network of correspondents set up around the country. There was news editor Michael Lawlor, assistant news editor Jim McElroy, sub-editor Eddie Cusack, and two reporters, Ned Power and Jimmy Moran, who spent most of their time in the Dail and Senate. I didn't know how the news was gathered and disseminated prior to this, until I found old bulletins in filing cabinets. They were paragraphs cut from the newspapers, pasted on to sheets of foolscap, and this was what the announcers – they weren't newsreaders or personalities – read over to listeners. There were three bulletins, at 1.30, 6.30 and 10.15 and with such a small staff the newsroom did really well. Inside a few years it gradually expanded as morning bulletins were introduced. Two roving reporters, John Ross and P.P. O'Reilly, were engaged as descriptive newswriters.

I liked working in radio. Everything had to be put in precis form and the reader had to be considered. Most of them liked to breathe, and alliteration in the bulletin could cause embarrassment.

Like all small organisations, Radio Éireann was a close-knit friendly sort of place, though the newsmen didn't fraternise much with the rest of the staff. I fraternised with anyone who was willing to fraternise with me and became specially friendly with Padraig O'Raghallaigh and Dermot O'Hara. We spent a lot of our free time walking and talking. Dermot had been in the Army Band and was certainly a captain if not a major when he fell down the stairs on the stage of the Royal during the *"The Roll of the Drum"*. He was an alcoholic and often told us of his adventures travelling with various shows as pianist for a few bob and a few drinks, as he put it, and playing the piano in pubs for drinks after he left the army. Dermot was a very talented musician, highly thought of by Brase and Sauerschweig and often conducted the Army No. 1 band before his fall from grace. He had been sober for some years before he got the job in R.É. as conductor of the Light Orchestra, which rapidly became a favourite programme with listeners. He wasn't reticent about his past, but he had put it behind him. One day, an ex-army officer saw him in the station and asked me if that was really Dermot O'Hara. "Last time I saw him," he told me, "was on the Curragh. Dermot was under house arrest and I was his escort. When an officer was under house arrest, you didn't guard him night and day, sort of thing, you just stuck your head in to his quarters now and again. When I went to stick my head in, Dermot was gone and the last I saw of him until today was him haring across the plains of the Curragh."

I lost track of Dermot after I stopped working for R.É. and some years ago I saw his death notice in the paper. He had a sharp tongue and wasn't the most gregarious person in the world, but Padraig and I enjoyed his company and his friendship. One of Dermot's great admirers and friends was Margaret Burke Sheridan, the world-famous soprano, to whom he introduced me. She was then an old lady but had a wonderful sense of humour and the verbal swordplay between the two always enthralled me.

Maybe my association with the broadcasting station was pre-ordained, for it must have been soon after it started to operate that I first came in touch with it. My father, then a flight sergeant in the Irish Air Corps, came home one weekend with what he called a wireless set. We didn't have even a gramophone at the time. The set had been made, I think, by a Sergeant Barnes, who also served in Baldonnel, and a strange-looking yoke it was. A small wooden box with a black top and a little pole sticking up at each corner, it was, with what Pop called a "crystal and cat's whisker" in a glass tube mounted in the middle. He strung what seemed like a hundred yards of copper wire around the walls just under the ceiling and after attaching one end to the set, plugged in four sets of headphones. After he'd scratched around a bit with the cat's whisker I heard a faint voice singing "Poor Old Joe." It was 2RN broadcasting.

When I worked there, I was intrigued whenever a fiddler was broadcasting Irish music: the producer always made him take off his shoe, and put a cushion under his foot, so the tapping wouldn't sound through the mike.

The announcers read news, cattle market reports, stock exchange prices and everything else, and there were times when I had to rush over to the Tower to recall one of the announcers to his duty, with a couple of minutes to go to news time. Time went quickly in the Tower.

Kathleen Dolan, a very lovely lady, was one of the announcers, and made history by using two words on the air which were never used in polite society nor even in newspapers until a few years ago. Once a month or so, a special correspondent sent in a general newsletter from one of the European capitals and the announcer read it out. It was just unfortunate that Kathleen was on duty the night the letter came from Paris. Listeners all over the country were stunned to hear: "And now, here is the French letter . . ." Kathleen didn't understand what all the fuss and sniggering was about.

Sport, which was always a great interest in my life, didn't figure largely on Radio Éireann until I took a hand. There were the GAA results read by Sean Ó Ceallacháin, on Sunday night, and there was "Soccer Survey" read by Bill Stanbridge, also on Sunday nights. There was also the racing notes on the Hospitals Trust-sponsored programme, the only sponsored programme put out by R.É. for many years, and there were commentaries on GAA matches by Micheal O'Hehir, and radio commentaries of horse races. One of the early racing commentators was known to have a little flutter, but the general public learned of his little interest when he was describing the finish of a race at the Curragh: "They're in the last hundred yards, Breakaleg is in front . . . Oh, Jaysus, he's beaten." It didn't go down too well with the bosses.

The result of an international soccer match in which Ireland was involved came over the agency wire one night, and I suggested to the boss we should stick it in at the end of the 10.15 bulletin, as there was a big interest in the game. In all innocence, he asked me "Is it a final or something?" to justify its inclusion. I decided there and then I'd do something about sports results, and without burdening the editor to make a decision, asked all our country correspondents to send in the results of any matches in their areas on Saturdays to be read after the 6.30 bulletin, and promised them half-a-crown per result. It was rather haphazard, but gradually most of them did send the results and that was the beginning of what is now a high labour-intensive segment of our broadcasting service. I was congratulated by the editor and promised his friendly consideration when he got financial approval for the appointment of a sports editor. But eaten bread is soon forgotten.

Years later, an advertisement appeared in the paper offering the job, and I duly applied, and equally duly was called for interview. It happened that three other applicants were waiting for interview after me.

I knew everyone on the board, the news editor, the Irish editor, the Director, and the producer of children's programmes, Seamus Kavanagh. I went through the usual motions although it was rather heavy going, for so far as I was aware, Seamus was the only one who had any slight interest in sport. The interview ended, and I was hardly in the corridor when Seamus came after me, inviting me to a drink in the Tower, whither we repaired.

The decent man called for the drink and then asked me, "Why didn't you tell us you were interested in the job? It's already gone." I can't say I was very surprised as I'd heard rumours the previous night in a pub nearby, and so I applied myself to the drink, putting out of my mind the thought of the other gobhawks waiting to be interviewed for the job that had already been given. I would, at that time, have preferred a job on news anyway. Some years later I almost got one, as I relate in another chapter. Still, I must have no pride, or else I'm very greedy, for when Peadar Keogh asked me to work in Montrose to cover President Kennedy's visit to Ireland for radio from the television, I did. Only for the money, I told myself. But even then the knife was twisted. Pearse Kelly, the Head of News in RTÉ was impressed by my work over the few days, and mentioned it to Peadar, saying I should be working for them full-time. He was taken slightly aback when Peadar told him I'd applied for a job, but hadn't been called for interview. I haven't worked for RTÉ since then. Has anyone?

I've worked for an awful lot of people and organisations, including two news agencies, both for a short time. Rushworth Fogg (that was his real name,) was features editor of the short-lived Irish News Agency and he commissioned me to do several articles for his firm, offering four guineas a thousand words. I did a few articles for Rushworth and looked forward to a long association and a profitable one, for four guineas was well over normal odds. It wasn't to be. The

INA had been set up by a coalition government and when that government fell, the News Agency was set down by the new government.

Anyway, what could the coalition expect? They'd set down the previous government's plans for a transatlantic airline by selling off the Constellations, so when the previous government became the current government the News Agency went.

It was a pity, as was discovered in 1969 when the trouble flared up in the North. The then government had to try to set up a kind of news agency, calling in public relations officers from various bodies, to make known the facts to the rest of the world. Even now, the paper wall of which Arthur Griffith spoke still exists, and we in Ireland are dependent on foreign agencies for news from other parts of the world, and agencies have their own viewpoints. With my hand on my heart, however, I can swear that the reports I sent to United Press for transmission to foreign countries were the truth, the whole truth and nothing but the truth. When UP closed their office here, Don O'Higgins, their representative in Ireland, asked me if I would be interested in covering sport for them as required, and once he was paying, of course I was interested.

The first marking he asked me to do was an international lacrosse match. I'd never seen a lacrosse, much less a lacrosse match, but that didn't stop me. With a lot of help from the people who stand around pavilions, and as it is a field game in which you can usually judge which is the better side, I did a creditable report and UP were happy. I did a few other events, usually international soccer matches, with the same effect and I wasn't a bit fazed when Don asked me to do a 1,000 word report on the Jack Yeats exhibition. There is some kind of artists' colony in Canada or Newfoundland or somewhere out that way, and the special report was required for the papers there. I knew Jack Yeats was an artist but as I can't paint even a blank wall, it was obvious I needed assistance.

Harry Kernoff was the obvious man. He was a real artist, even to the wide-brimmed black hat, and a nice little man at that, who was a regular at our sessions in Bill Aherne's Palace Bar. Harry was not a successful artist, financially; one time Kevin Collins bought a charcoal of a girl's head from him for about ten shillings when Harry was short of the readies, but he was respected in genuine art circles and I knew he'd oblige me. I picked him up at the Palace and at the exhibition not alone did he give me a condensed lecture on every picture but introduced me to Jack Yeats from whom I got a few words.

I was the star of UP stringers, even getting a bonus, and my association with them looked like being enduring and prosperous. I was covering only about half a dozen markings a year for them, but it was a nice little bit of crust, until the Germans caused my downfall. Not the nation, just some members of a party accompanying a boxing team. UP wanted a report on the tournament, and there was no better man for the job than Kelly. Next day, Don rang me, delighted, to say we'd beaten Reuters by an hour. The following day he rang me kicking up murder. He'd had a complaint from Germany that one of the boxers reported as taking part in the Stadium, had in fact been boxing in another part of Germany the same night. He was a champion of some kind. I couldn't believe I'd made a mistake of such proportions as I'd checked my programme with the announcements as the boxers came into the ring. Just to make doubly sure, I checked our daily papers' reports. They had the same guy boxing as I had. There was only one explanation I could see; the champion hadn't travelled and the German officials forgot to mention the substitution. At any rate, it shook my credibility, as the modern idiom has it, and UP cooled off me. It wasn't the end of the world, and my life went on as it still has so far, for, as I always say, every day you open your eyes in the morning is the best day of your life.

I've written millions of words, and been paid for most of them, yet very few of them stick out in my mind, though often when I come across cuttings of my stuff done years ago, I'm surprised at the quality. I don't think I could write as well today.

One piece, however, I do remember, though it consisted of only a few lines. I was reporting a soccer match every Sunday for the *Irish Press* and there were three teams in the league which were really terrible: Bohemians, Transport and Sligo Rovers. As two of them were based in Dublin, at least one of them was engaged each Sunday, and as I was not a staff reporter I was always stuck with the least important match. Invariably I had either Bohs or Transport to delight my Sunday afternoon.

Between the hoppin' and trottin', didn't the pair of them meet in Harold's Cross Park to set a new world record of boredom? I had time to count all moving beings in the ground and my report went something like this: "For a long time yesterday afternoon, I thought I'd got off the bus on the wrong side of the road for there must have been more life in Mount Jerome than there was in Harold's Cross Park. Including the officials, players and pressmen, there were 39 people in the ground, and a dog. The only real player I saw for the afternoon was one given to me by a colleague in the press box which I smoked. The result, predictably, was a scoreless draw."

Although Oliver had allotted nearly half a column to my

expected report, he let my offering go in full in the Monday's *Press*. It was to be expected that there'd be some reaction from Transport, and it came in the form of a phone call later that day from the secretary, who demanded an apology and appropriate action against the reporter. Otherwise, they'd withdraw their advertising. Faced with this ultimatum, Oliver rose to the occasion. "Please do," he told the caller, "I understand there are a few accounts outstanding." Perhaps it was cruel, but the human mind can stand only so much, and it must have had some merit, for the sincerest form of flattery was paid to it on odd occasions over the years.

I was proud to have ghosted the Nick Rackard story. (Incidentally, I much prefer to be a ghost than see one.) I have ghosted some other well known sportsmens' stories. There is a golfer whose story I ghosted for the English *People* and we've remained very friendly in the long time since then, and rightly so for the ghosting enabled me to persuade my bank manager to give me a badly needed overdraft and a furniture manufacturer to give me an equally badly needed dining-room suite.

When I had written the six articles, I sent a synopsis to the *People* and was more than astonished to receive a phone call from London a couple of days later. An English voice introduced itself as Jack Archer and, brisk and businesslike, he told me they'd buy the story. "I can only give you thirty," he said. I was silent, thinking five pounds an article wasn't anything like the vast sums the English Sundays were reputed to be paying for anything they thought would boost their Irish circulation, though it was possibly a tiny bit more than an Irish paper would pay at the time. Eventually I found my voice and repeated "Thirty?" "Look," said Jack Archer, "I'll go to thirty-five pounds an article and not a penny more. Take it or leave it." I hesitated only long enough to gulp and took it.

The letter confirming the deal came a few days later and Christmas was coming. The letter mentioned that the series would start in February and payment would be made as soon as the first article was published. I hastened to my bank manager, who had already reluctantly acceded to my pleas for an overdraft of fifty pounds which was still outstanding, and flashed the letter, urging him to up the overdraft to a hundred. He did, and a Christmas dinner was assured, though it looked as if we'd be eating it in the kitchen or if we wanted to be swanky, off the lino on the dining-room floor.

Ever resourceful – I hadn't been a Boy Scout for nothing – I dropped in on my friendly furniture dealer with the same act, and the decent man agreed to send out a beautiful suite of furniture for which I would pay when my Billy Bunter cheque came. More, knowing he was dealing with an honourable straightforward man, he knocked £25 off the shop price of £75 for me. So we did eat our Christmas dinner off a brand new dining table.

I hope I'm not risking jail and that the statute of limitations applies, for the fact is I was a con-man. My share of the deal wouldn't cover the two strokes I pulled, for the golfer had to get the lion's share. Nevenheless, as somebody said, sufficient unto the day is the evil thereof, and God never opens one door but closes another. The furniture man was paid off. And I'm still a customer of the bank, where, by the way I opened my account with an overdraft to finance my marriage, and was one of their best overdraft customers until a couple of years ago.

Martin Francis Coffey used say I was a very good creative writer; that episode inclined me to believe he was right.

Chapter 9

Medium Rare

Every year, a thousand school-leavers apply for admission to the College of Journalism, each of them having at least two honours in the Leaving Cenificate, one of which must be in English. Graduation from that College is one of the ways of becoming a journalist. Another is to know the right man. About twenty of them will pass the preliminary weeding-out process and at the end of the course, if successful, they will have a bit of paper which will entitle them to look for a job as a journalist. Journalists are different from ordinary folk as those who do enter the trade will discover. They'll be in a different world. It's a world where police never drive, walk or cycle to make an arrest: they always swoop. And though police don't usually have squeamish stomachs, they very often throw up roadblocks! Criminals never rob or steal. They invariably grab or snatch, and the proceeds must be quite weighty, for they never carry away the loot, they always haul it. Sometimes they carry out their snatches, hauls or grabs, with military precision. Anyone who has ever been associated with an army other than the Sally Ann knows that military operations more often than not end in cocks-up. Is this the newspapers' oblique way of saying the villains botched the job? Remember the removal of Nelson's Pillar from O'Connell Street? It was blown up by the ubiquitous person or persons unknown with little consequential damage. The army, with military precision, demolished what was left of the memorial, and blew out half the windows in O'Connell Street.

According to the media, rings of steel are thrown around with careless abandon, making no doubt a helluva clatter in the country, though in spite of this activity, people are being gunned down every day in the week, which apparently is a fate worse than being shot to death. Only the Irish are terrorists; other nationals in the same line of business are resistance fighters, freedom fighters, members of a liberation army or guerrillas, even those who committed the murders in Munich and Lydda. Terrorists operate only against Britain.

But it's comforting to know that sometimes police mount a full-scale murder hunt. There's a lot of taxpayers who would feel less than satisfied with a half, a quarter, or an Airfix-model-sized murder hunt.

Bishops, according to the media, have peculiar habits. They always rap or slate, or in particularly angry mood, lash out. Talk about being belted by croziers! Farmers' too, are an aggressive lot, for, according to the headlines, they never ask: they always demand. Pop stars and wealthy people don't travel like the rest of us. They jet all over the place. Just like the Mannikin Pis in Belgium?

The grassroots have withered slightly, and the dynamic wind of change promulgated by Harold Macmillan and fanned into a gale of hot air by our politicians and apprentice politicians, UDC, TC, UCC and MCC, has moderated, though there are still plenty of viable propositions in the country, and, especially during election times, there are so many swings you'd think Ireland was one grand carnival. Roll calls are no longer made. They've been replaced by head-counts, and, especially in political circles, the enumerators are nearly always tight-lipped. Perhaps they're accustomed to talking through their ears? Light is still found at the end of the tunnel, particularly at the end of the day, although the situation may be unclear.

It's obvious that the requirement for entry into the College of Journalism of an honour in Leaving Cert English is having its effect for one newspaper carried a headline referring to a "Grizzly Murder", while the story underneath giving the bear(?) facts made no mention of any animal being involved. Another headline informed its readers that Mr X "Excepts Offer" although in the story, the player had agreed the terms offered him.

Still I suppose one cannot be too pedantic about spelling – look at the way the British spell Chumley – especially when it's clear that the reporter who spelled "inadmissible" three different ways in the one report was giving everyone his choice. Although, according to one report, eighteen were lost when a ship "sunk", we haven't yet reached the point when somebody "done" something wrong in the newspapers. The day may not be far off, as already singular nouns – none, everybody, everyone and a few more – no longer govern the verb, and "none were injured", or "everybody did their own thing" are standard in the media.

Honours English has a lot to answer for. One of the gossip columns, written by a journalist who discreetly reveals that he has had the benefit of attending a third level educational establishment, reported that members of a certain organisation had accused its committee of acting partially. The members were quite right to be aggrieved, for any normal person would expect a committee to act fully. This columnist once told his readers that somebody had "betted" him something or other.

The sports columns can also emphasise the difference in world view between journalists and commoners. Some years ago, I read a report of a GAA match in the course of which the writer alleged that one player had hurled a minor over the bar. It was a cruel thing to do to a youngster. And in the report of a soccer match, the score line of which showed that one team had beaten the other by four goals, the opening sentence advised the reader to "ignore that scoreline". It puzzled me for days. If it was to be ignored, why was it put there in the first place?

A player named Fagan had a painful experience, according to one reporter. A goal came through him, and I winced in reflexive sympathy, as I once had a fork stuck through my fingers and still remember the pain. A "square ball with goal written all over it" kept me awake for nights. I know that a round ball is used in soccer, Gaelic football, tennis, lacrosse, hockey, cricket and hurling and an oval-shaped ball in rugby, but intensive research in the National Library failed to uncover any game played with a square ball, which must have been very difficult to control. And what was the esoteric significance of writing *goalgoalgoalgoalgoal* all over it and who dunnit? I'll probably never find out.

Just as managers have become an integral part of all team sports, slotting has become an essential part of their duties. Every week I read of a player being slotted into a position, though days beforehand he might have suffered the indignity of being pencilled in, and inevitably the ball is slotted into the net in three or four reports on Monday mornings. Particularly in Gaelic games, according to the media, mentors abound, so many it appears that there's one teacher for every player.

Unless they're all preaching the same lesson in the same way, there's bound to be confusion.

An item of intelligence in an evening paper, to the effect that Bohemians had good players in Smyth, Kelly and Burke seems to have passed unnoticed by the medical profession. Gynaecological history in the making, apparently. Another scribe informed his eager readers that Dublin should win because they had good players like Keaveney, Hanahoe and Doyle, but he kept their identity a secret, and I never discovered who were the good players like Keaveney, Hanahoe and Doyle.

In my time, I have seen many whiskey noses and porter bellies, yet I was a bit concerned and at the same time envious of the writer who attributed to a twenty-one-year-old footballer a rye smile. I was envious of the expertise which could pinpoint the type of whiskey which caused the smile, since the experts who can tell the difference between Jameson and Power by taste are highly regarded. I was concerned also that the player didn't buy Irish in this hour of our need.

It's well known that different newspapers have different policies, which can be reflected in their main headlines, as when the *Irish Press* proclaimed, "I am standing says O'Malley" at the same time as the *Irish Independent* announced, "O'Malley to run". And they can give the wrong slant by times. One daily paper was carrying a self-advertising display which listed its selling points as "The paper with the best sport", "The paper with the best adverts", and so on, with the punchline: "The paper you wouldn't miss"! Another very famous newspaper once announced its first prize in a competition as "A week's holiday for you and your wife in Butlins. Or a weekend for two in Paris." Presumably the alternative prize would have been presented in secret.

I've known a number of television and radio commentators

and some of them are nice fellows. Some are tolerably well-educated and can write their names. You'd never think in talking with them that they possessed supra-natural powers which are revealed only when they are working in their medium. No matter how far away the commentary box is from the action, the commentator always mystically knows just what the participants are saying and thinking. "Jones is saying to himself he won't get many more chances as easy as that," the commentator tells us, or "The ref is telling Smith to cool it, or his name will go in the book". He may well be high up in the commentary box in Wembley, Murrayfield or Croke Park but it doesn't matter. He knows what's being said, and he lets us know. Some of them know even what animals are saying or thinking. "Playfair is saying to himself, 'I'm not going into that stall'," one commentator told us during a TV visit to a racecourse.

All this really impresses me. As I've said, I've known some commentators and you'd think they were ordinary men, yet they must have some special powers. Is it extra-sensitive hearing, or extra-sensory power and is it a required qualification for a job as a commentator? – like a Northern accent?

Sometimes a racing commentator worries me for the afternoon by telling us, "It isn't raining or anything like that," for my mind is distracted from the real business to pondering what might be like rain and not be rain. I used to rack my brains when the commentator told us such a horse had won by the proverbial mile or with the proverbial ton in hand, trying to associate mile and ton with a proverb and the only thing I could come up with was the miss being as good as a mile, which didn't seem to relate. Anyway, after I'd heard it a couple of hundred times, I just ignored it.

Television inhibits the commentator from flights of fancy for you can see what's going on, and I have to admit I've been a little suspicious of radio commentaries for a long time. Once at a racecourse, I was standing near the commentator and a horse, I'll call him Bobskate, was thirty yards in front of his nearest rival as he came up to the winning post, when to my amazement I heard the commentator scream: "Coming into the last hundred yards, Bobskate's in front, but now Fastasleep's coming at him . . . he's gaining . . ." Bobskate had passed the post by this time. Another time I was reporting a match in England and the BBC commentator was sitting behind me. We were watching two different matches.

Media is the term used by journalists to describe collectively newspapers, radio and television. It is also the plural of medium, two dictionary definitions of which are: "Average, moderate" and "Person claiming to be a vehicle for spirits' communication with human beings".

Most times, the definitions seem pretty apt, though the newspapers have one redeeming feature over television. Apart from some by-lines, the newspapers don't give credit. You know the sort of thing that takes up five minutes after every presentation on television:

Produced by . . .

Directed by . . .

Commentary by . . .

Costumes . . .

Make Up . . .

Sound . . .

Vision mixer . . .

Production Assistants . . .

Wardrobe Mistress . . . and so on.

Just picture what would happen if after every item in the paper came:

Editor . . .

Chief Sub Editor . . .

Chief Reporter . . .

Reported by Sub-edited by . . .

Body type set by . . .

Headline set by . . .

Page made up by . . .

Proof pulled by . . .

Proof read by . . .

Plate made by . . .

Machine man . . .

Motor scooterist . . .

Sold by . . .

Chapter 10

The Day I Rescued Kippure

I couldn't really refuse to take part in the rescue of Kippure. It was March and the worst snow and frost for many years had made impassable the road up the mountain to the RTÉ transmitter at Kippure, and the technicians there were short of food and water. Efforts had been made to supply them by land, but a jeep had slid off the road into a ditch and had been abandoned; no other cars or trucks could get up the hill. And by all accounts, the situation was serious.

Then to the rescue, like the American Fifth Cavalry, came the Irish Parachute Club. That's how I became involved, for they invited me to a reception beforehand, at which they announced their plans, and at which, in the accepted and acceptable manner, refreshments were provided. For us, not the marooned men.

Later in the night, Peter, one of the prime movers in the club, invited me along for the ride, and, overcome by drink and emotion, I agreed. The drink had been flowing at the reception; the emotion came from loyalty. For hadn't I worked in the newsroom of Radio Éireann, for nearly nine years, on and off? And didn't it sound like the kind of sortie that might make a good story? Going home from the reception that night, nostalgia – and the drink – welled up in me. I had learned the craft of radio journalism in the newsroom. Many a time had I read over the bulletins to the Director of the Government Information Bureau for clearance before they could be allowed over the clear ether into the ears of the Irish people.

Assistant News Editor, Jim McElroy and I were the first to break the news to Ireland that Russia had sent Sputnik into space. It was on a Sunday afternoon usually a time when we'd be hard put to fill ten minutes for the 6.30 bulletin, and at first we thought it was a hoax as the story came over the teleprinter. But it wasn't, and after our bulletin we began to get calls from people who claimed to have heard what was to become the call sign of Sputnik: *bleep bleep.*

I had just arrived into the newsroom for my late shift on that February evening in 1958 when the unemotional teleprinter signalled "Flash: Manchester United aircraft crashed in the snow in Munich this afternoon. Many dead (more)." And as the reports came over the wires, I grew sadder and sadder as I learned that players I'd known and liked, and journalists I'd known and liked – Frank Swift, Henry Rose, Roger Byrne – would never again have a laugh and a crack and an argument with me. It was late, too late for the evening news bulletin when the printer told us that Liam Whelan was missing, believed killed. Whelan I had known since he played for Home Farm, and a few months earlier Man Busby had said to me: "In a year or two, that boy will be the best inside-forward in Europe." God decided otherwise.

I remembered too, how I had nearly become a staff man for the station. The Radio Service had advertised two vacancies for radio journalists and invited applications. Since I had been working in the newsroom for almost six years, often preparing the bulletins singlehanded, I applied for the job and was called for interview.

I knew I had a good chance, for there were very few journalists around who had radio experience, so I wasn't really surprised when, after a few days, the News Editor, Michael Lawlor called me into his office and told me I had come out on top in the interviews, and I had got the job. The other vacancy had been won by George Burrowes.

I was over the moon. The Radio paid over the newspaper rate; I knew and liked the work and considered I was good at it. Michael told me I'd start at £850 a year – big money then – that I could continue with my *Sunday Press* column so long as it didn't interfere with my radio duties, and that I'd get official notification inside two weeks. I woke my wife when I arrived home after midnight that night to give her the great news.

But a couple of evenings later, Jim McElroy called me out on our tea break, and over a drink broke the news to me that I hadn't got the job after all. He had been deputed to tell me, as we worked on the same shift. Boiling, I challenged Michael Lawlor. He told me he was sorry, but the civil servants who were running the station wouldn't agree to my appointment. Apparently they didn't agree to George's either, and since neither of us who had been first and second in the interview got the job, I have often wondered why they bothered wasting money on the advert and the interview board.

Jim McElroy and I had always been good friends and colleagues, and we never had a cross word, until after my chat with Michael, when I told Jim that I was finishing up that night. I wasn't going to work for them any more. Jim was dismayed. "But I'll be getting two new men who will be no good to me for about six months. I want you to stay on to train them," he complained. I may have been unreasonable, but I didn't.

I was still working in the newsroom when the television service was being set up. On the late shift, just before the 10.15 bulletin, a mill on Jones Road caught fire, the biggest blaze on the north side of Dublin in years, and I had done a good job on reporting it, getting the full story into the bulletin before it ended at 10.30 p.m.

To get from Henry Street to Jones Road, I had taken a taxi, for which Michael had given me half-a-crown expenses. Obviously I could make my own way back! Next day, he passed on to me a message of commendation from the newly appointed overall Head of News for my work. But when the television advertised for journalists with radio experience, I wasn't even called for interview.

On reflection, it was probably more the drink than the loyalty which caused me to commit myself to the mercy flight to Kippure, and on the Friday, the day before the big lift, with the drink long gone cold in me, I racked my brains to think of a way to avoid the flight. I couldn't think of anything, but craven desertion, and I was too cowardly to just not turn up.

The flight was scheduled for the afternoon. The frost was still heavy on the ground, and hard snow had been brushed off the runways of Dublin Airport, when I arrived at the far side, away from the terminal, over at the Boot Inn. Peter and the parachutists were in great form, putting supplies and barrels of water, with the addition of some stronger liquids, into packs, and attaching them to parachutes.

The mercy plane stood there, quivering with the cold, its fabric-covered wings and body every bit as frail as I felt. It was a twin-engined D.H. Rapide biplane, manufactured in 1936, years earlier. It was, I think, a ten-seater, but the seats had been taken out, except for four, to make room for the supplies, and fixed lines ran through the cabin, so the chutes would be opened as the packets were flung out. The door had been taken off to facilitate what was delicately termed the "drop".

There was a rather disconsolate little group of photographers huddled together a little way from the plane. Mick Loftus from the *Press,* God rest him, was there; Jim Mulkerrins the newsreel cameraman was there; and young Bodell – not old Cliff, nor even his son, but his grandson, Roy, who looked like a mere kid, was there too. Most newspaper photographers are nutters at the best of times. They'd do anything for a good picture, but even they didn't look too happy about the proceedings, though they were in a better position than I was, for they had been detailed by their papers for the job, while I, out of spite for my rigid upbringing, which had trained me to keep my mouth shut, my bowels open and volunteer for adjectival nothing, had volunteered. "God's curse on the drink", as the peasant said, when his hand shook as he aimed at the landlord and missed.

Anyway, I was stuck with it, up there in the freezing unfashionable far side of the airport, and they wouldn't even let me into the Boot for a quick one, because the plane was only waiting for a pilot to make a quick takeoff to catch the fast-fading light. Eventually Peter heaved me up into the cabin into a small folding seat right behind the pilot. The. photographers were put two on each side of the cabin. The bundles of supplies, treated with far more respect than we were, were carefully packed and hooked to the static lines.

Peter, who was in charge of the drop, climbed into the back of the cabin, and the tiny Rapide, quivering with fright at every gust of icy wind, looked lonely and out of date, like a senile grand-aunt kept discreetly out of view while the younger members of the family, the Friendships and the Viscounts gloried in their youth and vitality, close to the terminal building.

Dumb and numb with misery and self-recrimination, I huddled in my seat for what seemed an age. Outside, there was some kind of an argument going on about the pilot. Luckily, we didn't hear exactly what it was about, and eventually, a young fair-haired kid, with a shabby duffle coat, climbed into the pilot's cabin, juggled around a bit, and suddenly the engines burst into life.

Over the racket of the engines, I could hear him talking into the mike, "Testing, testing. One, two, three, four. Can you hear me, Peter?" Nobody else in the aircraft, least of all Peter, could hear him, I gathered, when I heard him exclaim "Bugger it, the intercom's gone." He wasn't going to let a little thing like that stop him for without warning the aircraft started to roll.

Accustomed to the swift rush of the Viscount down the runway, I thought the Rapide would never get off the ground. It was at least an hour, I'd swear, before she tore herself away from earth, supremely doubtful of her own ability to get into the air and stay there. So was I. Just when I thought I was going to be part of a Reuter "flash" and with visions of the headlines – "Six Killed Outright in Mercy Plane Crash into the Boot Inn" – the ground dropped away from our wheels.

It was close. There were telegraph wires and the roof of the Boot just below us, as the Rapide clawed agonisingly upwards. The duffle-coated youth was muttering strange incantations, no doubt a necessary part of the ritual of flying the prehistoric machine. I was silently saying seventeen decades of the Rosary. Mulkerrins, moustache wiggling, was taking sighting shots with his movie camera. Loftus and Bodell were checking their gear. Peter was sitting comfortably amongst the bundles, completely at ease.

I swear I'd have been in O'Connell Street quicker by bus,

for it was ten years of my life later that we passed over Nelson's Pillar, heading towards the Wicklow Mountains, grey and forbidding in the distance. We must have been all of 2,000 feet up as we passed over Lansdowne Road, and the sight of the players, wee dots on the green field, induced another surge of self-disgust at my idiocy, for I could have been sitting safely, albeit cold, in the Press Box beside Dave Guiney, from whom I might even have got a slug of Paddy. I vowed the next time he asked me to go to a Rugby match I wouldn't refuse, no matter what commitment I had made beforehand.

Soon, too soon, we were into the mountains, or rather, into the wall of fog which covered them. Through gaps we could see the unending blanket of snow which blotted out any vestige of green. The youth who was driving the thing dipped the wings so we could see. There was nothing to see, although at one time he pointed out the ice-bound road to the transmitter, elatedly indicating the overturned blue jeep which had failed its mission.

You couldn't talk with the noise of the engines, for which I was perversely glad, because I couldn't have said a word if it was to save my life. I was too busy praying.

Without warning, the fair-haired youth turned around to shout at Peter. Peter shouted back, but there was no sound. I screamed at the youngster: "For God's sake keep your hands on the bloody steering wheel!" He ignored me, and kept mouthing words at Peter. On cue, Peter rose and fumbled his way through the bundles. He leaned over to me: "Two minutes to the DZ," he shouted. I thought at first he had said, "Two minutes to the end," and renewed my fevered prayers. Then, from the numbed recesses of my mind I recalled that the nonchalant paratroopers in the war always shouted "Gung ho" or something equally idiotic when they reached the Dropping Zone. Hence DZ.

The DZ, as so often happened during the war, was locked in. Thick walls of fog covered the transmitting mast, all 300 feet of it. I thanked God. Now, we'd have to go home, and we hadn't been spattered all over the Wicklow hills. We might – just might – make it back to the Boot Inn.

But as our elders and betters used to say, "the mills of God grind slow," and anyway, my prayers were never answered quite in the fashion I hoped for.

Tipping way over on one wing, the youthful madman at the controls went down lower still and lower, unlike Keats' skylark, and it was quite impossible to determine which was the grey snowy ground or the grey fogged sky. It wasn't, however, impossible to see the malignant stay wires which, it appeared, held the towering mast in place on the top of Kippure, brushing the wing tips, ready and waiting to whip off the lengths of canvas-covered wood which held us in the air.

Peter was standing balanced like an old-time sailor rounding the Horn in a gale, at the gap in the fuselage where the door should have been. In sign language, he beckoned the madman at the steering wheel to go lower, and then frenetically began to heave out the yellow coloured packs. Forcing myself to look through the misted window, I watched as the red parachutes mushroomed into full bloom, gently wafting the food, water and drink – there's a difference between water and drink – to the tiny figures who burst out of the hut, waving gratefully to us rescuers.

Loftus, Mulkerrins and Bodell were happy as sandboys, banging away, or whatever photographers do, with their cameras. Each wore, instead of a face, a beaming smile. I closed my eyes, the better to make my prayers heard. A slap on the shoulder felt to me like the ungentle signal of Gabriel. Reluctantly and slowly, I opened my eyes to see Peter's broad grin framed by two upturned thumbs. My prayers turned from desperation to thanksgiving. Now we could head for home, and there seemed to be quite a chance that the staggering Rapide, having made it to Wicklow, would make it back to Collinstown.

But, as the Good Book says, or should say if it doesn't – blessed are they who expect nothing, for they won't be disappointed. Just as the duffle-coated youth had the plane straightened out and seemed to be trying to find his way out of the hills, the other three maniacs with cameras encouraged him to go down again, "just for one more shot". He didn't need much encouragement and he obviously fancied himself as a Stuka pilot. Pity he was too young for the war.

I screamed. This was tempting Fate in a big way. This had to be it. Those malevolent stay wires seemed to be grinning with satanic glee as not once more, but twice, the lunatic at the wheel dived low, trying hard to dislodge the ice from the stays, first with one wing tip, then with the other. My mind could take no more. Mercifully, it just didn't function. They say when death is imminent all fear goes, and a desperate resignation takes its place. I can vouch for that. I no longer saw the headlines. No more did I see in my mind's eye a few tiny piles of blood-soaked canvas and wood lying in the Wicklow hills for weeks before we could get a decent burial.

I came back to life as we recrossed Lansdowne Road. Astonishingly, though I had lived three lifetimes, the players were still showing their bottoms to the crowd in what passes as a rugby game.

The Rapide, to my amazement, was still chugging along through the air, both engines still working. The nut at the wheel was humming contentedly to himself. The Liffey passed below us, the North Circular Road, Drumcondra, Santry and then we circled the aerodrome, the roof of the Boot Inn welcomed us, and we touched down.

We taxied out of the way of aeroplanes, real ones, and with a last defiant blare – or the last gasp – the engines died.

I was last out of the plane. Not by choice. I just couldn't stand up. I joined the little group, all congratulating themselves, and with a sickly grin, I tried to look part of them. Peter, the instigator of my agony, came over, cheerful as Oul' Nick on his home patch when he gets a new shipment: "Just great, wasn't it? And Clive, the pilot was just super. He wasn't qualified on twin engines," he enthused. "Wonderful," I concurred. He thought I was talking about the operation, but I meant my safe return, and I wove my way into the Boot Inn.

Three whiskies later, I was able to go out to my car, a 1948 Ford Anglia, which gave marvellous mileage per gallon according to my friends, who had to push it to start, and after the usual manpowered switch was on, I was on my way home.

It was five miles to my home, and in my Anglia, it took me only half an hour. On the way, my courage came back, and by the time I came in the door, I knew I was a hero. I had paid my debt to Radio Éireann. I had enjoyed the trip. Guiney had been skulking safely in the press box while I risked life and limb for my fellow creatures. It was a great feeling.

I felt like Alcock and Brown, Fitzmaurice, Mollison and Lindbergh all rolled into one. My wife, who knew where I'd been, said: "Your dinner's cold, you bloody eejit."

Chapter 11

Public Relations

Butty Sugrue was only about five feet six inches in height. But he was, it seemed, about five feet six inches in depth, and about five feet six inches in width, which lent a certain degree of authority to his words. His claim to be the strongest man in the world was given an amount of validity by his feats of lifting and throwing prodigious weights, and was reinforced by his towing of a London double-decker bus by his teeth. I forget now if the bus was laden with passengers, but as this performance was achieved in full public view and featured on the newsreels, I was quite prepared to accept that Butty was, if not the strongest man in the world, at least a very strong man, one to whom a sensible man like myself, unequipped with a Sherman tank as a means of self defence, should accord a modicum of respect. So when Butty burst unannounced into the office of the *News Record*. which I was editing in the early fifties, I gave him a polite welcome.

The *Record* was the only newspaper circulating in Dublin, the others being closed by a strike of the printers whose union, the DTPS, was dissatisfied with their rate of pay.

Butty flattered me right off by addressing me by my first name, giving the impression that my fame had spread to far-off

London where he had a pub in one of the Irish enclaves. I learned afterwards he had got my name by the simple device of asking the first man he met in the printing works, yet his gambit put me in a receptive mood. He was promoting professional boxing in Tolka Park and he wanted the country at large and Dublin in particular to be made aware of his enterprise.

"Give us an oul' bit of a write-up, willya?" he asked, and invited me to lunch. It wasn't exactly the Hotel Russell, but at least I was saved the embarrassment of pretending I knew anything about wine, for Butty just grabbed a waiter by the arm – I thought later the poor chap might have been permanently disabled – and demanded "Two mixed grills and chips and two bottles of lager. And hurry up, willya?" He ate like a man in a hurry, explaining he hadn't had breakfast, having come by plane from London only that morning, and as he gulped he gave me a résumé of his early life, how he used chase goats in the Kerry mountains to drink their milk, and how he used to eat raw rabbits and other small animals when he was a boy before he ran away to become a strong man in a circus.

Now, I am as sceptical as the next man, but not by the merest shade of an eyebrow-raise did I indicate any trace of doubt of his story. Sceptical I was. Cowardly I was. But foolish I was not, and I stayed my oft-times rash tongue by stuffing the mixed grill and chips into my mouth *quam celerrime*, as old Julius was wont to describe the manner in which he despatched thousands of Helvetii in his Bello Gallico. The mixed grill was cooked, I hasten to add, lest it be thought that Butty had carried his undoubtedly healthy but somewhat nauseous boyhood eating habits into manhood.

Never a man to waste an opportunity, as Butty ate he was

regaling me with the story of his life, in the expectation, he said, that I would write it for one of the English Sunday newspapers, which paid remarkably well for a series. He also made it clear that his primary purpose was to get the "oul' publicity for the fights". Sporadic attempts had been made to popularise professional boxing here, without conspicuous success, and the business was not highly regarded by those who put any store on integrity. Indeed, the hurling of chairs, coins and other objects into the ring to the chorus of "Fix" was accepted as part of the spectators' legitimate amusement. Promoters had been known to disappear during the fights, and it was not unknown that some of the gladiators would end the night's endeavours minus their fee and some teeth. After Butty had made it plain to me that he was no fly-by-night promoter, being a good Kerryman, and interested only in putting the pro game here on a sound footing, I agreed to act as his public relations man for the sum of £20, which was slightly more than two weeks' pay for a journalist.

Like Jack Spratt after the sauce, Butty licked his platter clean, swallowed his lager, grabbed the waiter, studied the bill, paid it without too much rancour, gave me a handful of free tickets for the fights, hefted his suitcase, and, telling me he'd see me in Tolka Park two hours before the bill started, he departed. A little bemused, I finished my lager and went about my business.

During the week, I got some idea of how Jimmy Walker, Mayor of New York must have felt, as I grandly distributed free tickets for the fights, and on the big night, satisfied I'd fulfilled my part of the bargain, which was easy as we were the only daily paper, I arrived well before the first contest was due to start. Walking down Richmond Road, I felt great, being "Hallo Bill-ed" by a chorus of people, those to whom I'd given free tickets and those who hoped I had more to donate, and I was conscious of being clearly identifiable as a VIP when I bustled importantly into the office. Butty and his co-promoter were busy, he told me rather brusquely, and said he'd fix up with me after the show.

Professional boxing audiences then were pretty stereotyped. Bookies were always prominent in the ringside seats, and as well as the MC's, there were a few other dinner jackets on display in the front rows. Once or twice during that period, I seem to recollect an innocent or misguided Lord Mayor gracing the occasion, but generally the audience was made up of the lower order of sports followers, tic-tac men, and bookies' clerks, battered ex-boxers who always got in for nothing, and young men interested in Boxing who reneged the Stadium for the night. There were also some well-dressed young women accompanied by their fathers or uncles, and it was noticeable that the bloodier the contests, the more they shrieked with delight.

The bill went on, more or less as arranged and advertised, though a couple of late substitutions didn't please the crowd and some of those who took part in the fray obviously hadn't been within a mile of a gym in the preceding twelve months.

It was all good fun for the cognoscenti yet there are malcontents everywhere that you couldn't please even if you gave them your arse for a suckin' bottle as my granny used say in moments of exasperation, and it must have been some of that type who raised shouts of "Fix", "Cheat", "Robbery", "Give us our money back" and other unflattering slogans. A little uneasy, I gathered my cronies before the final round of the last contest and slipped down to the Widda Maher's refuge at the bottom of Richmond Road for light refreshments. Some time later, the publicity team, the two men who had plastered the city with bills, appeared, and in reply to my anxious inquiry, told me Butty and his co-promoter were to meet us in Harry Byrne's on the Howth Road next morning to pay out. Thus it was I made my way to Harry Byrne's, an oasis I seldomed, if that's the correct antonym for frequented, at an unseasonable hour. The publicity team was already there, both of them looking a trifle uneasy as if their ammunition was running low and the assault on the publican might falter for lack of material. Fittingly the Public Relations Officer gave these fieldhands a distant but friendly nod, and ordered his own drink. Their unease had transmitted itself to me, however, and fingering discreetly the coins in my pocket, I estimated I could afford a second pint which should allow me a total waiting time of one hour before Harry could accuse me of loitering. My time limit had not expired when I saw the look of relief on the faces of the publicity team as the co-promoter came through the swing doors. It was premature. He was expecting to meet Butty and return to London. We were expecting to be paid. He didn't and we didn't.

In a philosophical mood induced by a quart of porter, I wrote off the experience to experience, consoling myself that it hadn't cost me any money, which entitled me to membership of a rather exclusive club, and besides, I'd got into the tournament free, and for a brief hour I'd been a man of importance.

I didn't see Butty Sugrue for some years, though telephone calls from him in London came at odd hours of the day and night, and in the post, at infrequent intervals came letters containing newspaper cuttings and photographs: "Butty with Jack Solomons at the christening of his baby", "Butty with Jack Doyle", "Butty in his pub", "Butty Sugrue lifts a 15 stone man with one hand", presumably material for the story he wanted me to ghost, but I ignored it and after about a year he got the message for the calls and letters stopped.

In the meantime, Martin Francis Coffey, who had a publishing firm in College Green and for whom I wrote hundreds of thousands of words, suggested we should go into Public Relations in a regular way, it being, he deemed, the coming thing. Martin Francis was a man for whom I had a great respect and admiration. A true Christian, there wouldn't be enough stiles in the length and breadth of Ireland to accommodate all the lame journalistic dogs he helped, though little enough was the thanks he got from some. With Mick McInerney, Martin was one of the pioneers of the National Union of Journalists in this country, and with a few others, they brought that union from its knees.

If Martin thought Public Relations was an important sector of journalism, that was enough for me, and we agreed to form a company, bringing in Kevin Collins and Bobby Hopkins, the photographer. And so was born Public Relations Ltd, the first such Irish company in Ireland. We subscribed £25 each to make up the share capital of £100, and took offices in Earlsfort Terrace at a rent of £250 a year. The offices were furnished and carpeted by a friend on a sort of sale-or-return basis, our office acting as a sort of showroom for him, though I never heard of anyone rushing out from them to buy his produce. Our full-time staff was an intelligent young lassie as receptionist typist who got a modest wage, and we had stationery and prospectuses printed by friends. We were in business.

It wasn't long until we got some good accounts, AET and Smithwicks amongst them, and our first project for the brewery was a visit by some twenty journalists to the historic establishment in Kilkenny. The national papers, weeklies and magazines were represented and we laid on a full freeload which has now become the accepted practice of the better class firms. It had some interesting results.

The convoy of cars reached Kilkenny without mishap and the tour of the brewery yielded some good copy and pictures for the journalists. Of course they sampled the product, and the meal laid the foundation for later libations. All would have been well but that the head brewer, a charming old chap, had an interest in ancient Ireland. His researches led him to experiment with brewing mead, that drink for strong warriors which had as its base natural honey, and, convinced he had succeeded in brewing the real thing, he urged it upon us in generous measure. It went down like mother's milk, and assuming it had the characteristics of the original, its effect threw a bit of light on the reasons for some of the more exotic habits of the Ancient Gaels like slinging brainballs, one of which, thrown by an enemy, stuck in the forehead of Conor Mac Neasa, or scooping up handfuls of clay and flinging them around indiscriminately which led to the creation of the Isle of Man and Lough Neagh. Conor was a bit unlucky for he carried the brainball around in his forehead much as Dan Breen lived for a long time with bullets in various parts of his body, until Good Friday when the skies darkened and the earth trembled, upsetting poor Conor who started to shake with fury in frustration at not being able to prevent the Crucifixion and the brainball was shaken out of its place, and he dropped dead.

The mead didn't affect any of our party in quite that way. At least there were no new islands or lakes in the immediate vicinity, nor was there any report of a shaken out brainball causing the death of a journalist.

I summarily dismissed the claims of those of our charges

who arrived in Dublin at irregular intervals over the next few days that they must have been held captive by the Little People because they couldn't remember a thing after leaving the brewery. I put it down to excessive drink and congenial company.

The scattered return, however, was of great benefit to us, as the stories and features appeared over the next fortnight, a sustained publicity campaign which immensely impressed our client.

One thing which dogged me all my life was my date of birth. I was born at the wrong time. Just after I had started to work and could afford a holiday abroad in the Isle of Man or even Blackpool, a series of events occurred which the rest of the world thought was a global war, but we in Ireland knew was not a crisis, only an Emergency, and that put an end to foreign travel for another decade. In the sixties, the newspapers were full of the "Affluent Society", but before I could find an application form and a proposer, it had vanished. And I was over the age limit to join the Permissive Society. So it was with Public Relations Ltd. We were just that bit too early, and when I needed help, it came just that bit too late.

Public Relations was not understood by most Irish companies, nor indeed was the concept, though a few of the major organisations including Aer Lingus and C.I.E. employed P.R. men, and we had to overcome sales resistance before the needed half dozen business firms engaged our service. Even so, after fifteen months we were becoming well-known and were rapidly reaching break-even point. Then, Martin Francis had a breakdown; Kevin dropped out, and I carried on for some months, with a lot of help from the company secretary, Rebecca, but she also had her main job, and she was not in a position to assist in the field work. It was a crisis situation, for to keep the company going and to expand it, required at that stage, full time attention.

The problem was that the company couldn't afford another ha'penny at that stage and I, with a wife and infant son, a house and no furniture, had become addicted to the habit of eating, so in the words of that immortal seafarer, Captain Boyle, the blinds wuz down. We had no option but to hand back the furniture and the carpets, pay off the typist, and close the books and the office.

Anyone who has ever gone racing will know that obnoxious character who buttonholes you after the race with "I was lookin' all over for you. I had that winner past the post," though if you do meet him before the off he'll have you in the gutter with his tips. His counterpart, a genuine businessman of my acquaintance – and then as now businessmen, genuine or otherwise, who number me among their acquaintances can be counted on the fingers of one thumb – offered £1,000 for a half share in the company, a month later. It added salt to the wounds, for if this guy figured a half share was worth a thousand quid, Public Relations Ltd must have been a potential goldmine.

Yet, we had achieved something. We had made a start, and we helped in founding the Institute of Public Relations by sending a representative to the inaugural meeting with the very few other practitioners of the art. I believe it's very respectable and important now. We had also educated business to the benefits of public relations practice. And we had founded the principle of the freeload, which has become the centrepiece of all functions organised by pros. We regarded public relations as a constant liaison between producer and consumer working closely with the Sales Division, to publicise new lines or improved designs, or any newsworthy developments in the business, and to ensure that legitimate complaints by the public would receive attention. Now, Public Relations is publicity as an end in itself, and, as in Daniel O'Connell's domain where you couldn't throw a stone without hitting the head of one of his kin, now you can't throw a stone anywhere in the world without hitting a public relations officer of one kind or another.

The freeload has become a way of life. I estimate that the dedicated freeloader in Dublin can keep himself in free booze and food for five days a week, by attending three or four of the dozen or so freeloads which take place every day. They don't hold them on Saturdays or Sundays, but two days' rest for the stomach would be essential anyway. There is a drawback. The freeloader would have to eat sandwiches and savouries, and drink shorts, but as the Senator says, it beats working. Admission is free: simply mumble a name and the name of a paper or magazine to the pretty girl who'll be the receptionist and the PRO will gladhand you and show you where to get a drink. Anoraks and battledress jackets are now an acceptable form of dress, and since clients apparently judge the success of a "reception" by the numbers present no questions will be asked. There will be a few journalists sent by their papers or magazines on the remote chance that something newsworthy may be said. The rest will be there for the beer. Experienced freeloaders usually stick with their normal tipple. If they're pints drinkers and pints are not available, they stick to bottles, but learners or gate-crashers, normal pint drinkers, tend to go for brandy or strong whiskey because it's free. And unless they're silent drunks, draw attention to themselves and may be blackballed.

One client I had, as I continued in public relations after the firm closed, didn't have any money for freeloads, and even if it had, wouldn't. It was the Association of Combined Residents Associations. I was their first P.R.O. and a pro, being paid two guineas a month for publicising the activities and trying to encourage other Residents Associations to come into the fold. The *Evening Herald,* which published the ACRA notes, paid me an additional two guineas for supplying them with the news. There came a time, however, when the Association could no longer afford me and we parted. But I can justly claim some part in the growth of the organisation.

For love of sport, I became the P.R.O. for the Olympic Council's fund-raising drive in 1964, to defray some of the cost of sending the Irish team to the Tokyo Olympics. Since the O.C.I. is an amateur body, I was an amateur, and like the gaining of the world at the cost of your soul, it profited me nothing.

It was my (honorary) office of Public Relations Officer to the Judo Association of Ireland which brought me into the Olympic Council's ambit, and it also brought me in contact with a real live commercial P.R.O. Seamus Kavanagh, Ireland's first Judo Black Belt, who was and is a friend of mine and he had a high opinion of my expertise in the publicity field, so at his urging, I agreed to take the job, and put judo on the Irish sports map. I'd always had an interest in the sport, anyway, and when we wanted to hold the first Irish championships in the National Stadium, I approached another friend, Pete McGlynn, who used have an accessible pub in Stoneybatter but who was at this time a big wheel in a brewery, for financial help.

Pete persuaded the brewery to give us the needed £250, and to arrange a certain amount of publicity for the championships, which also involved the holding of a press conference. The public relations officer would look after it.

Although I had no active part to play, with a few of the J.A.I. officials I arrived early in case there were any little difficulties to be ironed out, but as time moved on, and on, and passed the kick-off hour, there was a singular and noticeable dearth of journalists. Three quarters of an hour later, there still wasn't a journalist in sight, and the sponsor, if not exactly agitated, was palpably restive. The P.R.O. was fretful, and drew me aside to whisper, "For God's sake, can you do anything?" He didn't really mean for God's sake, he meant for his own, but as I wanted publicity for my association, I went and made a few phone calls.

Dave Guiney was sports editor in the *Irish Press,* so I rang him. I begged him to dig his off duty staff out of Mulligans or the White Horse and order them over here where they could have free booze, and by the way, to get a reporter along to cover the event. Mitchel Cogley of the *Indo* got the same pleas, as did Gerry Noone at the *Times.* And right nobly did they respond. Within 15 minutes there was as big a collection of sports journalists as you'd find in Croke Park on all-Ireland day. It was a great success. The sponsor was delighted. The Judo Association became known. The journalists enjoyed themselves. The P.R.O. was so relieved that he hated my guts for ever after. The worst thing you can do for some people is a good turn.

Dave Guiney dropped in on his break, and with a Paddy in his hand buttonholed me, waving the letter of invitation under my nose. "A right cock-up you made of this," he challenged. Indignantly protesting my shining innocence of any part in the arrangements, I read the letter. It invited the papers to send a reporter to the press reception all right. But it had omitted the date and time!

It was perhaps two years later I got the assignment which

caused me to opt out of public Public Relations and confine my activities to private public relations for personal friends. Phil Donoghue, who had been house manager of the Theatre Royal before J. Arthur had caused that temple to be rededicated from Terpsichore to Mammon, had set up as a theatrical agent after the closure. A very good friend of mine, and patently a man of discernment, Phil wanted me to handle the publicity for a roadshow in which he was involved. Without hesitation or discussion of terms I agreed, which once more proved that if not exactly a congenital idiot, I should almost always be accompanied by a minder, for at the meeting with the producer/financier, I was confronted by a former client and debtor, Butty Sugrue.

Almost the first words he said to me were: "Don't tink I've forgotten that twenty quid" and with a grandiloquent wave of his arm added he'd fix up for the two jobs together. Astute businessman that I was, I did rapid sums in my head and shot in a demand for £80. With that look of mutual respect which passes between two financiers at the conclusion of a satisfactory deal, Butty spat on his hand and crushed mine in testament of our agreement, and got on with the business.

It certainly looked as if Mr Sugrue was on a winner this time. By some mysterious means, he had got Henry Cooper, British and European heavyweight champion, to top the bill. Henry would do a training routine and a bit of shadow boxing. Jack Doyle was the second lead, and Phil Donoghue's job was to provide the supporting acts, dancers, a comedian and some music. The tour was to start in Dublin, cover the south and work its way up to Galway. I stipulated I'd handle the publicity, for Dublin only, my commitments, I said, didn't permit me to accompany the entourage, and this was the only titter of sense I showed in the whole affair. Everyone knew

Henry Cooper, the Mr Nice Guy of professional boxing, who was probably the most popular boxer in these islands. He was to knock the immortal Cassius Clay off his feet in a real contest, and though he got a bit of a thumping from The Greatest afterwards, it did his image no harm at all in the European boxing world. Jack Doyle was better known. A native of the Holy Ground in Cork who had taken up boxing in England, Jack's escapades were legion and highly publicised, and parents had handed onto their children and they to their children expurgated tales of some of his exploits. Jack was a boyo and even the straitlaced who didn't approve held him in affection.

Publicity wasn't going to pose any problems on this one. It would be the easiest £80 I'd ever earned.

Like many a good Corkman before and after him, Jack Doyle had joined the British Army, the Irish Guards, a few years before the War, and being a big fellow, also because sportsmen in armies got plenty of concessions, he took up boxing. He clattered a few fellow Irish Guards and sundry members of lesser regiments to become a champion, thereby attracting the attention of some shrewd promoters who saw his commercial potential. Tall, broad-shouldered, good looking with black wavy hair and a wicked glint in his blue eyes, Doyle wasn't a bad pugilist, and he had a pleasant light tenor voice, admirably suited to "Mother Machree", which he was prone to render at the end of his fights. The publicity machine got hold of him and built him up, on a carefully selected diet of hams, as a fighter, who could "box like Dempsey and sing like McCormack", which, after the notorious Phil Scott fight led one cynical sports writer to describe him as a boxer who could fight like McCormack and sing like Dempsey.

Jack didn't mind. He had women of all rank falling at his

feet, and inevitably Hollywood grabbed him. He had a great time there, he told me afterwards, and acquired two millionairesses as wives – at different times – and a number of mistresses. As everyone knows, booze, birds, and boxing don't mix, and Joseph Aloysius Doyle, as he appeared on the charge sheets before minor courts, was prepared to drop the boxing from his way of life. He made a lot of money. And spent it like water.

I met him first when I was an habitue of the dog tracks, consorting with a couple of trainers and others concerned in that rather seedy sport, as it was regarded before the setting up of Bórd na gCon. As always, I was brought into his company in the train of some friends, one night at Shelbourne Park, and since there never was a sporting event of any kind in this country which was brought to a proper conclusion without a liquid inquest, we ended in Paddy Burke's pub on Burgh Quay, where the results of that night's meeting were evaluated, winnings counted or losses bemoaned, and the following night's races analysed.

Joseph Aloysius was the centre of interest, and when he intimated he had some pressing business to attend to, and invited us to come along, we crowded into the taxi he'd summoned. First stop was McGoldrick's in Drumcondra, where he excused himself and left us in the pub. He was back inside the half hour and the taxi tour continued to Marino, where he left us for another 30 minutes or so, and his third stop was in the North Strand where at least we were able to while away the minutes in Berminghams. With Jack back, we finished our odyssey in a now demolished licensed premises in Lower Gardiner Street, run inevitably by a Tipperary man, and where we drank unhindered into the big hours of the morning. There were strict legal opening and closing hours, but they seemed to apply only to respectable people. It was freely suggested in the company – and not denied – that Jack had been visiting lady friends during his three absences.

I certainly wasn't a bosom or boozin' pal of Jack Doyle's. His standard and pace of life was far from mine, and as I had to earn a living while he just lived, we met only briefly and infrequently, in bars, in bars on racecourses, and at dog tracks. In one of his "going-well" spells, Jack Doyle decided to become a racehorse owner, and bought Pelorus from Bertie Kerr, one of the most respected men in the racing and blood stock business. I learned long afterwards that the cheque for £1,200 was 18 months old before it was finally cleared, but Bertie had a grádh for Jack and was tolerant. So far as I remember, Pelorus never won in Jack's colours though after he'd had to sell him to cover training bills, he won several races, including an Irish Lincoln at the Curragh. That may or not have been the day I last met Jack, but it certainly was on a Saturday, a Curragh day, that our paths crossed before he left to take up more or less permanent abode in England.

I happened to be passing the G.P.O. when a taxi pulled up right in front of me, and Doyle, resplendent in a camel hair overcoat, emerged, grushing pound notes. Everyone in Dublin knows what a grush is, but if there are any who don't, it's the time honoured social custom whereby the winner at a pitch and toss school, or the male participant in a marriage, throws a handful of coins in the air to celebrate his good luck, and the onlookers, usually kids, dive to grab the money. As he grushed, Jack bellowed "Jack Doyle is back in the big time!" and dragged me unprotesting into the nearby Princess Bar, now alas the prosaic and unromantic British Home Stores. The first man we met there was Ernie Smith, one of the classiest boxers Ireland ever produced, who made the lightweight title his own for many years. Too late he turned pro with a conspicuous lack of success, though as he told me, he never got hurt, and made a few pounds when he needed them. Jack was throwing the party, and we knocked back a fair number of bevvies – the accepted parlance for drinks in our circle, coined from beverages, I believe, by tic tac men who conduct their affairs in a series of contractions – and the talk was of booze, birds and racing. The party ended when Joseph Aloysius stood up and announced to the assembly: "Doyle is back on top again, and he's going to the only place for a man at the top, London." He caught the B & I boat, and that was the last time I saw him until Butty Sugrue brought him back into my life. Ernie and I continued bevvying and chatting, though at a much slower pace, until closing time.

Now Jack was back again, and I knew between him and Henry Cooper it would be easy to let the world know about Butty's roadshow. I set up the inevitable press conference in the Red Bank – it wasn't a church then, of course – and before that I had arranged an appearance on *In Town Tonight,* a radio show compered by Niall Boden, an old friend from Radio Éireann days.

Since everyone who had a wireless set listened to *In Town Tonight* I was reasonably sure the centres of population which were to be visited by the roadshow would be made aware of that attraction. I gave Jack an outline of what to say and I knew Niall wouldn't ask him any embarrassing questions, but most of all impressed on Doyle under pain of worse than mortal sin, the need to stay sober for just two weeks. That would be "no trouble, no trouble at all," he assured me. "I take very little now, and at my age, a little is enough."

His performance in the studio was magnificent. He was calm, confident and suitably subdued, and if he did depart

131

from the script, it was only to reveal that while on tour he would be looking for a promising young heavyweight, whom he and Butty would make into the new Jack Doyle, and aware of the pitfalls which had bedevilled the original, the second Jack Doyle could be guided past them and the sky was the limit. Which wasn't a bad line at all.

After the interview we came down into Henry Street, and Butty, ever mindful of his investment, wanted to call a taxi to take us to the Red Bank, but I vetoed the project. "Let him walk over," I counselled, and I was right: with Doyle towering head and shoulders over me, and head and body over Butty, we made a royal progress down O'Connell Street, and the crowds stopped and cheered and "Good Oul' Jack"-ed all the way. Dublin knew Jack Doyle was back. He got a great reception too from the journalists and I hovered around him like an anxious guardian angel, afraid he'd hit the bottle. I needn't have worried. Jack stood quietly, sipping a tomato juice, chatting amiably with the Press, sticking to the pre-determined line and throwing in the occasional quotable quote of his own. He kept his tomato juice glass full.

Knowing we were assured of acres of good copy next day, I was happy as we sat down for a meal, long after the freeload had ended. The Red Bank was a great place for steaks, and Butty, in expansive mood after the success, had ordered steaks all round. Before we sat down, he half turned his back on me, like a farmer about to buy an animal in the market, and peeled off a couple of notes from his wad, sticking them into my inside pocket with a mutter and a telling wink.

During the meal, I noticed that Doyle's eyes were a bit glassy and his speech slightly slurred and thought, "he's really past it, he's had only two small ones since the reception and he's half shot". But Jack wasn't all that far gone. He guessed what was running though my mind and grinned: "There was vodka in the tomato juice, Bill. I've been through all this before, with the highest paid public relations in the world trying to stop me." Oh, well, I felt, he'd done his act and it had gone over well, though at the same time I congratulated myself on having opted out of the tour.

The first show was in the Mansion House and though there was a fair bit of paper, as they describe free tickets in the theatrical trade, there was also a good number of paying customers. I was mooching around P.R.-ing as required, and Butty was standing at the door keeping an eagle eye on the cash desk, as the show proceeded. Henry did his bit of training and shadow boxing, the dancers danced their few steps, the musician muzaked and the comedian told his few jokes. Jack took the stage to a great ovation, gave a bit of patter and announced he'd sing his favourite song, "Mother Machree." He forgot most of the words, and tapping his chest apologised for a bit of a cold, then tried "The Holy Ground" with more or less a similar result. The crowd was indulgent, and if the show wasn't quite up to the standards of the old Royal, it wasn't too bad, and everyone seemed satisfied, particularly those who had free tickets.

In a quiet moment during the show I had sidled up to Butty. Since he was near the cash desk, I reckoned I had a good chance of getting my money, for I'd discovered the notes he'd pushed into my pocket totalled only twenty pounds, the amount of the original debt. Quite boldly I asked him for my sixty, to settle up, and I took him by surprise. At that very moment, the malevolent fate which had dogged me all my life intervened. A gate crasher had got past the cash desk and slid in through the double doors. With one hand, Butty grabbed his lapels, lifted him a foot in the air, and before I could say

Jack Robinson or an Act of Contrition, opened the doors with his head and flung him bodily into the foyer. Without even drawing a deep breath, the only sign of tension was that the bottom of his nostrils had turned white, he turned to me with just a slight trace of impatience, and asked "Dja tink I'd cheat ya ouruva lousy sixty pounds?" I did, but I wasn't going to tell him that, and adopting the better part of valour, backed out of range, dumbly shaking my head.

Later he told me he'd pay me in the morning as I'd have to be present for the grand departure.

I was there early, but not early enough. Butty was already in the car jammed between a mass of luggage and bodies and couldn't be reasonably expected to be able to get his hand in his pocket. Jack Doyle shook hands with me, complimenting me on the job I'd done by saying that never in his career when the highest paid P.R.O. in the world had handled him had he got two pictures in the one paper on the same day, one on the sports pages and one on the news pages in the *Evening Press*. It was a nice compliment, but I'd rather have had the money. Phil shook hands with me and told me not to worry, he'd be settling all the bills when he got back. I felt great sympathy for him, for he was a really nice man.

For the next few days I scanned all the papers, including the provincials but there wasn't a mention of the touring show, nor was there any tale of a new Irish heavyweight having been discovered, and like the dog at his father's wake, I felt a bit glad and a bit sorry. I was sorry the show was apparently not a roaring success, and I was glad they'd all now know that if they wanted publicity, they'd have to get the right man. Me. Then I remembered. They'd had me. About a fortnight later, I got a call from Phil. He sounded like a man suffering from severe shock, and from his rather garbled account I gathered that on the first stop, Jack had hit the bottle and tried to break open the young dancers' doors during the night which didn't please either them or the hotel management. There was some mix-up over the halls, and the caravan had broken up in disorder. There was also a number of bills outstanding. Between the hoppin' and trottin' I didn't get to meet poor Phil before he died in a car crash, and I never did get the full story. Nor my fee.

I never met Jack Doyle again. Someone ghosted his story in the *Sunday People* (for the second time in twenty years) a few years later, and in the episode I read, Jack described his attendance at the funeral of Dolly Faussett. Dolly was a café owner whose premises at one time was the resort of a number of ladies of the night, and a place where you could get a drop of firewater after hours. Jack had been a frequent visitor. The article was headed by a picture of Jack Doyle wearing riding breeches slow-marching after Dolly's hearse. His explanation was that was the only outfit he possessed, but I wondered.

I never met Butty again. He, like Jack., has passed on. With his innate flair for publicity, however, Butty made the headlines just after Nelson's Pillar was removed from the Dublin scene. The admiral's head, or more correctly the head of the admiral's statue, was missing. It turned up in Butty's pub, the Lord Nelson, in far-away London. My £60 never turned up.

They say Public Relations is a great trade, or perhaps profession, for meeting people. They say also that if you work for nothing, you'll never be idle. And balancing one tenet against the other, I decided to leave the field to those more fortunate people who don't seem to attract the same kind of friends and clients that I did.

Chapter 12

Nick

Since I came to the use of reason, I stopped taking the *Reader's Digest*. Really, I suppose, it was because I was becoming a hypochondriac. I mean, one month, I'd have all the symptoms of a hole in the heart; the next, it would be a hole in the head. There was always some medical diagnosis, so I stopped taking the magazine. There was one feature in it, however, which always interested me, "The Most Unforgettable Character I Have Met", and while I have met many characters who are supremely forgettable – most of them unfortunately just won't allow themselves to be forgotten – there are two people who left a lasting impression on me.

One was the late President de Valera, and I met him only once. In my time I've met some famous people, yet I can truly say that the much abused term, personal magnetism, was, to use his own words, an empty formula, until I experienced it from him. Dev was a man either loved or hated in the immediate post-Civil War period. The Soldiers of the Rearguard and their families idolised him. The soldiers of the Free State Army and their families hated him with a fierce passion, and the common people of our area of Dublin, and at the time there were very few aristocrats in the whole of the country, were certainly not amongst Mr de Valera's admirers. I'm sure most of them went to their graves without ever having seen him in the flesh, yet, mainly I suspect because their masters said so in the strictly controlled press during the Civil War, they all believed that Devil Éire, as they pronounced it and meant it, had started the Civil War. The kindest description they gave him was "that Spanish twister". His policy of neutrality during the World War undoubtedly ameliorated their feelings, but it was the passage of years which transformed antipathy into apathy. Indeed it is only in the last ten years or so, with the dying out of the participants, that the Civil War divisions in the country have also started to die.

As a child, and knowing no better, I believed Dev had started the Civil War. During my schooldays, I still believed it though by that time, I didn't care much either way. The Christian Brothers who did such a good job in educating those who are now said to be cherished by our Constitution equally with those who could pay for Belvedere, did not go into the niceties of the Treaty or Document No. 2, and our standard book of Irish history, *Stair Seanchas na hÉireann Cuid 11,* in the now forgotten cló Gaedhalach ended with: "I 1916, bhí. . . Éirigh Amach." It wasn't until long afterwards, when I had studied the history of the revolutionary period, that I became aware of the very minor part he had in the Civil War. In a way, Dev's contribution to the country was that of a figurehead rather than a man of action, much like Churchill was to the British during the Second World War.

As an orator, he left much to be desired. Of course, I had heard him speak many times at the Monster Meetings at the GPO during the very entertaining elections in the thirties, when we kids always went downtown to partake of the excitement, including heckling, fist fights and baton charges, which were an essential part of election campaigns. Television has taken a lot of fun out of our drab lives. Dev droned on, eh-ing out of him after every couple of words, in what seemed to me a dull monotone. There was no doubt, however, about the esteem in which his supporters held him.

It wasn't until 1948 that I met him face to face. He had been to some meeting in Strasbourg – it has been a favourite place for Irish politicians for a long time – and I was sent from Radio Éireann to interview him on his return. With a gaggle of other journalists, I was on the tarmac waiting for him when his plane arrived, and we all duly interviewed Dev.

I have forgotten the object of the meeting in Strasbourg but I know that I asked Mr de Valera if it was a success. He was standing within three feet of all of us and when he started to speak, I got the feeling he was talking to me only, that the others were being ignored, that there was nothing more important in the world at that moment to Mr de Valera than that I should be made fully aware of everything that had happened at the meeting. The modern expression "vibes," vibrations, most accurately describes the relationship I felt with Dev for those ten or fifteen minutes. I felt a warmth, a charismatic glow which emanated from him and enveloped the two of us to the exclusion of the others, and in fact, the rest of the world. I'm sure the other reporters felt exactly the same, as we took our shorthand notes of the clear concise explanation he provided.

It was only when I got back to Henry Street and transcribed my notes, that I found Dev had not uttered one unequivocal statement. Everything he had said was circumscribed by conditional clauses, and I had the utmost difficulty in writing an intelligible report to fill the half-minute's air time allotted to the report. I couldn't very well hand the report into the announcer saying, "Dev bewitched me," could I? He had. And it was only then, nearly half a century after the Civil War, that I came close to understanding the idolatry with which he was regarded in the early years.

My relationship with my other unforgettable character was of longer duration and was uncomplicated by vibrations or influences out of the ordinary. Nick Rackard was a very ordinary guy. So ordinary that it was in the Boss O'Connell's White Horse I first met him. He was with his brother, and I was with Dave Guiney, that man who has been the catalyst to so many of my misadventures, and we were all doing earnestly what most people did in the Boss's establishment: drinking.

Nick had pursued this occupation with more diligence than most for years before he accepted the fact that he was an alcoholic, and yet in those years he became a giant on the Gaelic football and hurling fields. With his brothers, Bobby and Willie, he brought his native county, Wexford, to the pinnacles of glory, ensuring for himself an immortal place in the records of the GAA. He was to Gaelic games what George Best was to English football, the difference being that Best earned vast sums of money from his talent, and Rackard, an amateur, drank vast sums of money which he was earning from his profession of veterinary surgeon. There was also the difference that the Irish newspapers did not record Nick's exploits with the same gleeful extravagance as the British papers did Best's. The good people of Wexford and the malicious, however, were not in ignorance of his escapades.

It took him twenty years and a half dozen sojourns in hospital to finally accept the fact that he suffered from alcoholism, and in that time, his once-prosperous practice was in ruins, his farm neglected, and his relation with his family strained almost to breaking point.

Slowly very slowly, the Irish are beginning to recognise alcoholism as a disease, like cancer or tuberculosis, though God knows, TB, before and for sometime after Noel Browne, was regarded as a shameful disease, on a par with VD, not to be spoken of outside the family circle. Even today, the Irish speak of cancer in hushed tones, dropping their voices and referring to it as "The Black Man" or "The Big C". Many still look over their shoulders when speaking of someone who died from "the-cancer-God-bless-us", giving the impression they regard the prayer as an incantation which will protect them from the evil. Alcoholism is incurable, and it can be arrested only if the patient wills it.

When Rackard became sober, and stayed sober with the help of Alcoholics Anonymous, he was in the rural equivalent of the gutter.

When he started to rebuild his veterinary practice he couldn't afford tyres for his second-hand car. Fortunately for him, a friend had been put off the road for drunken driving, and lent Nick the tyres off his immobilised vehicle. He put into the reconstruction of his life the same energy and determination he had put into his football and hurling. His family, like those of all alcoholics, must have been suspicious and fearful in the early days that the reformation would be temporary only, but Rackard got on with the job, and it was permanent. As well as rebuilding his life, he spent a considerable amount of his spare time travelling all over the country to AA meetings, to help other alcoholics by word and example. He thought nothing of driving through the night to Dublin or other distant towns to aid an alcoholic who needed help badly.

Inside a few years, he was prosperous and life was good. A thirteen-stone six-footer, though his weather-beaten face was more that of a farmer than a philosopher, Nick Rackard lived by the code of AA, which is essentially simple Christianity: "Make reparation for the wrongs you have done: live one day at a time. Subdue your aggressions and resentments. Harm nobody intentionally, but do good whenever you can. And put your life in the hands of a Higher Power, whether your conception of that Higher Power is a Christian God, a Buddha, or an Infinite Spirit." Rackard didn't preach. He practised. And he was no mealy-mouthed do-gooder. Except that he didn't drink, he was an ordinary guy, who talked the same as any ordinary guy, and could tell a bawdy story with the best.

Little more than a year before he died, at the age of 54, Nick Rackard agreed to tell his story through the *Sunday Press,* and I was his ghost, so I met him often over a period of months. Eighteen months earlier he had had an operation for cancer; some months later he had another, and while we were writing the story, he was undergoing radium treatment at St Luke's Hospital.

I've met a lot of people who have "looked into the lonely places", who have come face to face with death and known they've had only a short postponement. You can always tell it from their eyes. In moments when the guard is down, you can see the eyes look on the lonely places, fleetingly perhaps, but discernibly. I saw it in Nick Rackard's eyes, and he knew I saw it. Usually he talked about life, and how it should be lived. One day the subject of death came up, and I asked him was he afraid of dying. No, he answered. He didn't fear death, though he didn't want to die: there were so many things to be done. "It's funny," he said, "many times when I was drinking, I wanted to die, to end all the misery, but I was afraid. Now, I don't want to die, but I'm not afraid of death." Those who have looked at the lonely places are far more conscious of the

142

swift passage of time than those who know that death must come to everyone except themselves. There isn't a moment to be wasted. Nick was sad that he had had only six years in which, as he put it, the sky was bluer and the perspectives sharper, after twenty years in a shadowy world of unreality: six years to live and help others to live.

The Nick Rackard story appeared over four weeks in the *Sunday Press* and caused a sensation. Never before had an Irish public figure exposed his life to perhaps a million readers each week, admitting his faults and his alcoholism. It certainly wasn't written for money. Rackard took a long time before he agreed to do it, and then did it only because he felt that some alcoholic somewhere in Ireland might be helped. I know at least five who have recovered as a result of the Rackard Story.

Not long after the series had finished in the *Sunday Press,* Nick went into St Vincent's Hospital for the last time. When I visited him, it took me some time before I recognised him. His burly body had shrunk to less than seven stone. His face showed the indelible wrack of pain. Withal, he was cheerful and serene. He died a few days later.

Shaw it was, I think, or maybe Wilde, who said the Irish are a very fair race: they never speak well of each other. Nor, it may be added, do they ever tell the truth about themselves in public. Nick Rackard did.

When he died, the *Sunday Press* asked me to write an appreciation. They thought enough of it to put it on the front page, and a number of people congratulated me on the writing. For myself, I knew it was inadequate. I should have written it better for he deserved better, but at least it had the merit of sincerity. Nick Rackard deserved that.

Chapter 13

Boozing with the Borstal Boy

Boozing with "Borstal Boy" Brendan Behan called for the thirst of a camel, the stamina of an ox, the stomach of an ostrich, and a neck like a jockey's buttocks. There are still people alive in Las Palmas, Paris, London, New York and Toronto who can testify to that statement. There are even some alive in Dublin, Behans native city, who have survived the tidal wave of boisterousness and booze which was Behan on the bash.

In the capital cities of the Western World drunkards cheered and social drinkers marvelled at his Gargantuan appetite for drink, and the amount of noise and commotion which could be generated by one wild Irishman on the rampage. They saw him only after he had become famous, and presumably, rich, and many accused him of deliberately fostering the image of a beer-swilling bookwriter to boost the sales of his works. They wronged the man. He drank because, as he put it, "he liked the bloody stuff."

In fact, at the time he hit the headlines for his antics in New York and Toronto, Brendan had lost his fine edge as a drinker. He got drunk quickly and easily, not showing any of the form he had before the success of *The Hostage*, *The Quare Fellow* or

Borstal Boy, when we had to work hard for our drinks in Dublin.

That was towards the end of the 1940s when we were both writing as little as we could for as much as we could squeeze out of anyone who would buy our stuff. We always managed to find money for booze somewhere, and sure, if we didn't earn it honestly, some of our friends were sure to have money – the only problem was to find where they were hiding. We weren't exactly the most popular visitors to Dublin bars at the time, for Behan never entered a pub – he burst in behind his belly and a blast of noise, crashed through the swing doors, roaring out a song or spewing out a torrent of words. And barmen shuddered because the evening peace was shattered. And our friends shuddered because they knew that if we had no money, we'd borrow from them, and if we had money, we were bound to involve them in a booze-up. And some of them felt that Brendan Behan was the re-incarnation of the Devil, determined to lead them from the straight and narrow, down to the murky depths of an alcoholic hell. Many respectable hard-working journalists and genteel would-be writers gave us money just to get rid of us. To Brendan, the end, not the motive was what counted, and we accepted largesse from all who were foolish enough to offer it.

I became involved with the ex-Borstal Boy through an innocent liking for the drink. I had known him as a kid when we lived near each other, but when his family moved out to the council-house suburb of Drimnagh, I lost all trace of him, and didn't even connect him with my childhood acquaintance when I saw the report in the newspaper that he and another man had been sentenced by a military court to imprisonment for shooting at a policeman after an IRA funeral. The other man, incidentally, had also been a schoolboy friend of mine.

Years later, John Ross, the thriller writer, invited me to a party in the Catacombs.

The Catacombs was a peculiar semi-subterranean warren of rooms in Fitzwilliam Street, which was occupied at different times by various artists, writers, painters, and what have you. So far as I could figure, this party was being given by the Hon. John ffrench.

Only for the fondness for drink that was on me, I wouldn't have gone, for I guessed I'd be out of place. I was, too, for the company was arty. There were artists, writers, sculptors, musicians, dancers – even a journalist or two. Perhaps by a very loose interpretation of the word I may have qualified for this latter category, as I had just sold two articles to the *Evening Herald* for two guineas each. I discovered later that I was no more phoney than most of them there, for as invariably happens in Ireland, the wish was taken for the deed, and most of the writers didn't write, the sculptors didn't sculpt and the artists didn't paint. I don't know about the dancers or musicians – they didn't prove or disprove their claims, they just drank and talked.

George Morrison was there, but that was before he had proved himself with the film *Mise Éire,* and unless I'm mistaken Hoddie was there. Hoddie laid claim to no profession, but in fact he was a brilliant musician and a linguist, and that was as much as almost anybody knew about him. If "Mick" J.P. Donleavy wasn't there, somebody gave him a blow by blow account, for he portrayed all the happenings graphically in his *Ginger Man*.

Knowing only John, who had left me to my own devices, I got myself a drink and sidled over to a sofa, which backed onto another kind of sofa, and I buried myself in my tumbler. Behind me on the other sofa were two women, one of whom said she was a Russian, and a spy for the Russians, as well as the IRA, but I didn't believe her. I think she was just drunk.

All was going well in a haze of booze, cigarette smoke and noise, when the door burst open and there were men-and-women-girlish cries of "It's Brendan," over which rasped the coarse hoarse tones of your man: "Givvus a drink for jaysake."

The jacket was flying open, the shirt unbuttoned to the navel, the pants held up by a necktie, the hair was standing wild on the Nero-esque head as Behan followed his out-thrust belly, in the wake of his full vocabulary, over to the bar.

The self-alleged Russian spy said to her girlfriend: "That's Brendan Behan, he's delightfully coarse, don't you think?" and the friend concurred: "Ooh yes, chahmingly gross."

But Behan had no time for small talk. Straight from the door he headed, over to the well-stocked bar, a trestle set in the corner. He poured himself a drink, ignored the three or four people who crowded chattering around him, and fixed his bleary gaze on me. I hardly recognised him, after all the years, and his unwinking stare unnerved me slightly, for I feared he was going to denounce me as an interloper.

Then he bellowed: "Hey, Kelly! Come over here and have an effin' drink for jaysake."

I went. He told me he remembered me from Russell Street, poured me a drink, and made an announcement to the company.

"Now lissen, all yis," he said. "I'm Brendan effin' Behan, or if yis want to be nice, effing Brending Behing, an me and me pal Kelly here are goin' to drink. Any of yis that wants a drink, effin' get it yourself."

So Brending Behing and I settled down to the serious business of getting sozzled, me half terrified of this wild-looking character who bore no resemblance to the skinny snotty kid I had known nearly twenty years earlier. So completely had I lost track of him that I didn't know he had been sent to Borstal for carrying explosives into Britain, or that he had been interned in the Curragh as an IRA man.

Had I known, I would have been whole terrified, but since I didn't, and the booze was free and flowing, I settled in with him. He started off by asking me did I know the Bourkes. Of course I did, the theatrical costumiers and producers – everybody in Dublin knew the Bourkes. Rich, they were said to be.

"They're cousins of mine, but they don't want to know me, I'm not respectable," growled Brendan. "Someday they will. Someday they'll be glad to know effin' Brendan Behan." He went on talking, hopping from one subject to another – the Aran Islands, the tenements in Dublin, snatches of Gaelic, a bar of a song. He talked of painting – house painting – "I'm a painter, you know, just like effin' Hitler, but I'm not startin' any wars, I've had enough." And he kept on talking, until between the drinks and the splatter of words and subjects, I drifted into an alcoholic euphoria. Brendan's face swelled and shrank, swayed and faded, appeared and disappeared, but the barrage of words kept battering against my ears, no longer intelligible to me, but somehow hypnotic, in the hoarse beery voice with the slight stammer that got worse as he got excited. Mechanically I kept on drinking. It seemed to me that the drink was having no effect on Behan, though looking back on it, he must have been getting crocked too.

How it ended, I don't know. About 2 a.m. I staggered out through the door and into the dark street. Nobody missed me. Nobody came to see if I was alright. So far as I know, Brendan Behan was still knocking them back. I know I got home, for I found myself in my own bed next day with the father and mother of all hangovers.

It was three o'clock that afternoon before I felt well enough to struggle to the bus stop, on my way into the city, to see what was doing, but primarily to have a curing hair of the dog. I had the bus fare, a few cigarettes and the price of a drink, and as I waited in silent agony for the bus, a familiar hoarse voice broke in on my headache.

It was Behan. Behan on a bicycle with one pedal, no brakes and one mudguard over which was strapped what looked like a bundle of dirty white rags.

"How the jaysus hell are yeh?" was his greeting as he flung down the bike and threw himself on the grass verge. "Givvus a fag for jaysake," he asked.

We sprawled there smoking my cigarettes, the back wheel of his bike still idly turning. No word of last night's booze-up passed between us. Real drinking men in Ireland don't talk about last night's session, and Behan was a real drinking man.

We were in Whitehall, a suburb on the north side of Dublin, about ten miles as the crow flies from Brendan's suburb of Drimnagh, though why any discerning crow would want to fly the ten miles to find exactly the same neat rows of identical council houses is something I have not yet figured.

"What are you doing out here?" I asked, more for the sake of conversation than information.

"They're building down in Artane," he told me, "and I'm goin' there lookin' for a job. I'm a painter y'know, a effin' good painter. Here's me brush, and there's me overalls on the bike," pointing to the dirty white rags strapped on the mudguard.

"Surely you don't expect to get a job at this hour of the day. Surely you'd have to be down at eight in the morning for that?"

He screwed his big head around to look at me pityingly. Dimly I wondered if the effort caused him as much pain as it did me when I tried it.

"Sure that's why I'm goin' down now. The Union sent me after the job, and the oul' fella is givin' out to me for not working, so I have to go. No effin' foreman in his jaysus senses is goin' to give me a job at this hour. I don't want a job, but I have to go after it – go through the motions anyway."

We smoked in silence for a while. Then he got up on his bike, and with a "See you in the Palace tonight", he was off after his no-job.

The Palace was one of his favourite haunts. Though he frequented the "intellectual" bars like the Pearl, Neary's, and Davy Byrne's, where James Joyce used to drink, Brendan was more at home in the Palace, run by Tipperary man Bill Aherne, or the Boss O'Connell's White Horse, or even more so in the bars around the markets. These had an added advantage. They opened at seven in the morning. In the following months, he introduced me to them.

At any time of the day, morning noon or night, there were old women sitting sipping their glasses of porter, good women and not so good women, but they were all the same to Behan. He knew them all. "Ah, Maggie a stór, how the hell are yeh? Julia me oul' darlin', have a jar and give us a bar of a song." They all knew him, too, and because he was one of their own, a Dublinman, they loved him. He spoke their own language. And when he bought them a glass of stout, the benedictions flowed like holy water over his unruly head.

"The blessin's of Jaysus on yeh, Brendan, me oul' flower. May yer shadda never grow less. Shure it's yourself is the heart of the rowl."

Brendan, in what passed for sotto voce for him, would give me a potted biography. "Maggie there – ah, an oul' star. Great woman she was durin' the Troubles. She used hide the guns under her skirt when the boys had carried out an ambush.

Bejaysus, shure even forty years ago, no Tommie was goin' to look there for a gun."

Or: "Julia? An oul' toff. Thirteen kids she had. God only knows who's the father of half them, I'm sure she doesn't. But she'd never see yeh stuck for a bit or a sup, no matter where she got it."

And then he'd burst into song, roaring out a Dublin street ballad, the veins on his neck swelling with the effort, his head cocked to one side, eyes downcast, face getting redder and redder as he bellowed out the words. Gradually the age-cracked voices of the oul' wans would chime in, until at last the long-suffering barman would hammer on the counter with a plaintive: "Now, gents. Now ladies, pleeuse. What about me licence? What about the law? Ah gents, ladies pleeeuse . . ." He wasted his time. Once started, there was no stopping Behan, or the oul' wans, for that matter, and the concert usually broke up with us being asked to leave. And not come back.

In any event, we'd have to go, because the money would be nearly gone, and we'd have to make our way down to the Palace or the Pearl and put the bite on someone for more drinking money.

In the White Horse, we would sometimes be lucky and meet Benedict Kiely, the novelist and writer. Ben would always stand us a few drinks and Behan and himself would get into a deep and learned discussion on Irish ballads. They seemed to know them all between them. Ben with his clipped Tyrone accent would sing a few bars, and Brendan would be waiting his turn to break in with "one I heard in Kerry this summer".

And the owner of the pub, the Boss O'Connell, that silent Limerick man, may the good Lord rest him, would be standing behind his bar with never as much as a shush out of him to the singers. Rarely, only rarely, would the Boss admonish us, and then it would be with a gentle "Now, Brindin, now Bill, don't you think you have enough?" We never had.

The Hostage, The Quare Fellow, Borstal Boy, "Brendan Behan's New York" – they were all in the future, lurking somewhere at the back of Behan's massive head.

I was doing a minimum amount of work which left me with a maximum of time, and Brendan was writing casual articles for the *Irish Press* – little gems they turned out to be – and the combination was dangerous. We met three or four times a week for drinking purposes, and invariably ended up by doing the Stations of the Cross, as Behan called it, crawling from pub to pub. We were never really too broke to drink. If I hadn't a friend I could tap, Brendan had.

Looking gloomily into the dregs of our glasses in the Palace with no sign of relief forces arriving, Behan would suddenly burst out "Ah, eff this. Come on, there's a fella up in Neary's who'll give us a pound." And there always was. People were always glad to help him out.

One regular source of assistance was Eamonn Martin, a friend of Brendan's, who was always good for a pound, but we'd have to go up to Baggot Street bridge to ambush him at a certain hour. There might be a verbal struggle for a while, but Behan always won. Yet, even armed with money, we couldn't make straight for the nearest bar.

"I'm barred there – and there – that hungry effer barred me last week for singin'. He's so miserable that if he owned Switzerland he wouldn't give you a slide."

To Brendan, the worst crime a man could commit was to be "miserable" – his word for a tightfist – and any "miserable bastard" who wouldn't buy him a drink when he needed it, was left in no doubt about his rating with Brending.

A few months of this kind of life brought my bourgeois instincts surging to the surface. Besides, through some peculiarity of fate, I had got a regular sports column in a Sunday paper, and was getting offers of work at feature-writing. Behan, too, was getting restless. He'd drag me from one bar to another for no reason, and we'd abandon that after a short time for yet another. "Doin' the stations," he'd grin, baring all the two teeth in the front of his mouth.

Looking back now, I guess he was beginning to realise that he had to write something more lasting than the brilliant little vignettes he was doing, and deep down inside him, he knew that so long as he stayed in Dublin he'd be on the merry-go-round and get no serious work done. Benedict Kiely claims that Dublin is the hardest place in the world to do any writing. He confided in me once when he was on holiday that between O'Connell Bridge and the White Horse bar, a distance of less than 75 yards, fourteen people invited him to have a drink.

Behan's restlessness broke to the surface one afternoon as we sat sipping beer in the Palace bar. He was moody and less talkative than usual. Without warning, he finished his pint and said: "Eff this. This is a dead jaysus hold. I'm off to France. Slán agat." And off he went.

Like the dog at his father's wake, I didn't know whether to be glad or sorry. On the one hand, I'd miss the quare fellow, the excitement, the new faces, the roars and shouts of him, the flow of gab that made it unnecessary for me to try to make intelligent conversation. On the other hand, without his disturbing and disrupting presence, I'd be able to do the work I was offered, make a bit of money and buy clothes as well as drink. I was always bourgeois-minded.

Of course he came back. I was standing idly in Westmoreland Street, mentally debating whether I'd go to the Pearl or the Palace, when he appeared from nowhere. Behind me I heard the voice "Bill, me oul' flower, how the hell are yeh?"

"Come on around to the Palace and buy us a pint for jaysake," he bellowed. "I'm effin' parched after drinkin' that bleedin' frog wine for months."

In Bill Aherne's Palace Bar, he told me about his sojourn "on the continong". He had been picked up and jailed in England, because he was still an undesirable person after being deported on his release from Borstal many years earlier. Eventually, he got to France, with nothing in his pocket, but that never worried Brendan Behan.

"Ah, here and there, pickin' up a bit now and again," he answered my query as to how he lived in France. "I wrote a bit of pornography for some frog publications," he chuckled. "Bejaysus, it's lucky no one in Ireland will see it, or be able to read it in French even if they did see it, for the confraternities and the sodalities would drown me in holy water, swimmer an' all that I am."

"I mooched around," he laughed, "and when things got real rough, we used to touch the pilgrims. Begod there was a million Irish pilgrims going through Paris on their way to Lourdes – I suppose they wanted to see a bit of wickedness before they got caught up in the blazin' fervour of their religion at Lourdes. But they were a miserable hungry lot. It was terrible hard work to get the price of a drink or a bit of bread and cheese outa them. All their effin' charity must've been reserved for buyin' candles at the shrines."

Behan was back. And we were off on the roundabout again. Once more we did the stations – the Pearl, Neary's, Davy Byrne's, Keating's, the White Horse, until finally I staggered out of a bar somewhere in the Coombe, leaving Brendan amongst a crowd of the oul' wans he loved, roaring out street ballads like the Bull of Bashan.

He didn't stay long this time. Soon he was gone again, and I was relieved, happy to get back in my little groove, writing my column, doing a few features, having a quiet drink, and working on the Great Novel – which hasn't yet been finished.

Many weeks later, I was working in the radio station when doors started to open and slam in the corridors and a hubbub of voices rose to crescendo with one very plain, very definite Dublin accent overwhelming the others. It was the Quare Fella himself. Unfortunately for Behan, however, the noise served advance warning of his coming, and producers and directors took to the hills, before he could crash in on them demanding money.

Along the length of the corridor I could hear, "Ah, Mr Behan, ah now . . ." from the attendant, drowned by Behan's roar "Will yeh for jaysake leave me alone. I'm only lookin' for the money yis owe me, yis miserable shower of bastards."

Brendan could never get it into his head that the rules of the radio station demanded that payment for items could be made only at the end of the month. I was pressed into service "to get him out of there for God's sake".

Eventually, he came out with me, albeit reluctantly, and then only on condition we went for a drink. We did the stations again that night.

But I was as much a Peter as the rest. Some time later, I was waiting for my date in Westmoreland Street, when even the roar of the traffic in that busy thoroughfare couldn't drown the roars of Behan from the far side of the street. "Hey, for jaysake Bill, wait for me. Don't get on that effin' bus. Wait." Brendan, waving a walking stick and hobbling across the street, stopping or dodging the speeding traffic, caught me before I could flee.

"Look, for jaysake," he bellowed at the top of his voice, "Sean Kavanagh's walking stick. I broke me effin' ankle in the Joy and the dacent oul' fella lent me his own stick. I should have given it back to him when I got out, but I still have it."

Brendan had been lodged in Mountjoy prison after an altercation with the police, and Sean Kavanagh, the governor, lent him the walking stick. Incidentally, he never got it back.

"I'm after bein' over at the Press and up in your place and over in the *Times*, trying to get some bleedin' money off them and I can't get it!" he bellowed. "Come on an' buy us an effin' drink."

Brendan was never a modest violet. Still less did he care for convention, and people were stopping to look at us, thinking a fight was going to break out. I cringed, afraid my date would come along, and the good impression I had carefully fostered would be shattered. As rapidly as I could I whisked him around the corner into the Palace, bought two pints, gave him five shillings, finished my drink, and muttering something, dashed off, ten minutes late for my date but with my façade of respectability intact.

A week later, coming from the cinema with the same girl, I saw a commotion starting at a political meeting at the corner of Abbey Street, and heard Behan's stentorian profanity rising above the jumble of noise. Doing a rapid about-face, I wheeled her across the street and home.

My third betrayal came a few weeks later, on a Saturday night. I was working in the *Sunday Press,* and on "cutline" was going for a drink in the Scotch House. One of the reporters stopped me: "Behan's up there at the corner of Hawkins Street, maggotty drunk, fighting with a policeman." And I turned on my heel and went around to Mulligans, cursing myself for a coward, for I might possibly have got him away from the policeman quietly. If I had I would have saved him an appearance in court.

Our paths didn't cross often after the success of his plays and *Borstal Boy,* though the book was banned in Ireland. Occasionally we met in a crowd in the White Horse, but we didn't get much time together. He had money now and he was drinking more than ever, yet he was no fool. One sycophant asked him for an autographed copy of *Borstal Boy*.

"Certainly," replied the Quare Fellow, "buy the effin' thing and I'll autograph it for you for nothing. How the bleedin' hell do you think I'm goin' to live if I give a copy free to every moocher in Ireland?"

On another of the rare occasions on which we met, we were in Tommy Moore's pub in Cathedral Street. Two people from the radio service were with us, and naturally a few acquaintances sat near us, joining in the conversation drawn by his reputation. When it came to Brendan's turn, he asked in the approved manner "What are yis havin'?" One of the acquaintances opined he'd have a pint, and Behan rounded on him. "Who the effin' hell are you?" he asked. "I didn't ask you into our company. Eff off and buy your own drink"

The news that Brendan Behan had been married surprised a lot of us. I had never seen him making up to any young girl at parties, hoolies or in pubs. He had always concentrated on drinking and was somewhat less than civil to unattached young women. Only with the oul' wans in the market pubs had I seen him comfortable. I didn't quite believe he had married until once more on a Saturday night I slipped out of the office for a drink and I met him and his wife walking along Burgh Quay. "Meet my effin' first wife, Beatrice," he roared.

"Beatrice, this is me oul' china Bill Kelly, one of the effin' best."

Beatrice, a small dark quiet girl who spoke only when spoken to in company, was to all appearances the most unlikely mate for the rumbunctious Brendan. Even in her presence, his string of four and six letter words flowed freely, but the marriage was very happy.

Between his marriage and his trips to Europe and America, I didn't see much of Brendan. Once he stopped me to ask me to give his uncle a mention in my sports column. The uncle had been managing a junior soccer team for thirty years, said Brendan "and never got a shaggin' mention from anyone". Flattered that a famous figure like Behan should ask me, I obliged, and next time we met he bought me drinks and thanked me.

Rarer and rarer were our meetings, but the change in him was apparent. I could see he was dying. Each time, he was a little more sunken, a little more vague, and the light in his eyes was slowly but surely going out.

The last time I saw him was shortly before he died. He was in Tommy Moore's pub in Cathedral Street with another man, a stranger to me. Behan was standing at the counter, shirt and pants pulled over his pyjamas, the big wild-haired head of him canted to one side, the eyes dull and unseeing.

I called hello to him and he slurred, "Who the effin hell are you?" Then as I came closer, he recognised me: "Ah, Bill, how the hell are yeh? Have an effin drink. I ran out of the hospital for a jar — I couldn't stick it any more." But I refused, had my own drink and went out.

I could see the death in him, and he refusing to accept it, as if he believed that by standing in a bar as he had done so many times, he could keep the Reaper at bay.

It was a funny kind of parting from me "oul' china", the

Borstal Boy who had grown up to be a patriot, a gunman, a playwright, a writer, and one of Dublin's characters, a fellow about whom more legends have grown up since he died than about Fionn Mac Cumhaill himself.

He died in March 1964. The world and his mother were at the funeral. The people who had run out of bars when he arrived were there, talking, telling of their intimacy with Brendan, the genius of him that they had recognised under all the coarseness and profanity for which they had forgiven him because he was a genius.

They boasted at the funeral, too, about their times with him, the Peters who didn't want to know him before he became famous, and who avoided him when he was drunk, which was often, or when he was broke, which was often, too. They were safe now. Brending Behing was dead.

We Irish are good at the *nil nisi bonum* trick. Our cemeteries are crowded with "horrible dacent fellas who'd give you the shirt off their backs". That's when they're safely dead. When they were alive they were boozers, bowzies or bums to be avoided by all right thinking people.

They were at the graveside, the ineffectual intellectuals who could boast about knowing the Borstal Boy because no longer need they fear that Brending effing Behing would burst into a pub behind his belly and his stream of profanity to upset their cozy abstractions.

They were at the graveside too, his friends, the oul' wans, the cabbies, the dockers, and the few genuine friends he had in literary Dublin.

I didn't go to Glasnevin. I knew there'd be enough there without me. Instead, I went into Tommy Moore's pub and had "an effin' pint for jaysake". My boozing with the Borstal Boy was irrevocably finished.

Chapter 14

A Man of Vah'lence

He was in his middle sixties when I first met him, a smallish man dressed in a shabby dustcoat and trilby hat, greasy with the dirt of years. A small military moustache neatly trimmed adorned his upper lip, in a rather pathetic effort to preserve the memory of his youth and his rank of commandant in the infant Free State Army. His spectacles were pebble-thick and he walked slowly, with the aid of a walking stick.

It was almost impossible for me to visualise him as his revolutionary comrades knew him, young, dapper, wearing a bowler hat, lavender gloves and a blue nap overcoat, with a badge in the lapel proclaiming it had been given by his Britannic Majesty "For Loyal Service".

This man had never served his Britannic Majesty. As a youth he had joined the Irish Republican Brotherhood, and as a young man he had been a killer, had shot spies, touts, suspected spies and members of His Britannic Majesty's armed forces in Ireland.

He had sworn fidelity to an Irish Republic, but, I think, his overriding loyalty, like that of the Irish tribesmen of ancient times, was to his Chief, Michael Collins, Director of Intelligence of the Irish Volunteers, who master-minded the guerrilla campaign which achieved more in less than three years than any of the risings and rebellions in the previous three hundred years. The Tan War, as it is better known than the War of Independence which respectable people call it today, set the pattern for modern guerrilla wars, and, as well as starting the break-up of the British Empire, gained independence for five-sixths of Ireland. Joe Dolan, the shabby little man I knew, took full part in that war. He shot and killed people in cold blood. He was one of Collins' Intelligence Officers, part of the secret service set up by the Corkman that outwitted and outfought the British Secret Service, which, since its foundation by Walsingham in the time of the first Elizabeth, was and probably still is, one of the most effective and ruthless arms of government in the world.

It was forty years after he had put away his gun that Joe Dolan talked freely of the men he had killed. He told me of the shooting of "Jameson", the British agent who got closest to Collins, up near the Albert College in Ballymun. Jameson was an Irishman named Burns who was serving in the British Secret Service. Posing as a jewellery salesman, with a hobby of breeding canaries, Jameson took up residence in the Granville Hotel in Dublin, and proceeded to worm his way into the confidence of those close to Collins. He promised to get pistols and ammunition for the IRA, but eventually he was uncovered and orders for his execution were given to the Squad, as Collins' hand-picked special unit was known.

Dolan's story goes: "Paddy Daly and some others collected Jameson by appointment and brought him to Ballymun in the tram, under pretence of meeting Mick Collins. When we arrived at the lonely lane, we told him he was to be executed, and told him if he wanted to say prayers, he'd better start. He was a brave bastard. Instead of saying prayers, he said: 'You're making a big mistake. Mick will be mad when he hears about this.' Daly hit him with a thirty-eight, and the bugger kept on walking. So I hit him with my forty-five and he dropped. We went off and left him there."

Joe told me he was detailed to search Jameson's room, but there was nothing incriminating to be found. He took a case of jewellery samples out of the room, and having, he said, pocketed a few pieces from it, he dropped the case into the Liffey.

He was one of the party who shot Alan Bell, the bank inspector who was sent over by the British government to try to uncover the Sinn Féin fund accounts, and he was getting warm. Too warm, so the Squad was once again ordered to "hit" him.

Dolan's story: "One of our men followed him from Blackrock where he had got on the tram, and others were waiting in Ballsbridge for our man to come and tell us which tram. Our man arrived, puffing and blowing and we got on the tram, two up front on top and two at the back, and some men downstairs. We weren't sure of Bell and we kept saying 'That's the favourite for the two-thirty', and things like that. Eventually we took him off the tram, holding up the passengers, and shot him in the street. We parted, and I got the tram to Ellesmere Avenue off the North Circular Road where I lived then."

Collins had ordered the elimination of the British undercover ring of agents in the city on Bloody Sunday, November 20, 1920. Joe Dolan was one of a party which was to get a Lt. Noble in Rathmines: "That was the name he was going by at the time, but these fellows used different names for different days of the week. We burst into his flat, but he wasn't there. Whether he had been tipped off and got out in time, or whether he was out on a job, I don't know. His fancy woman was in the bed, naked. We would have shot her, but we didn't have orders to, so I turned her over on her face, and took a bayonet out of a scabbard which hung over the bed, and gave her a couple of skelps with the flat of it on the arse, and we left." The porter in the Wicklow Hotel wasn't so lucky. Liam Tobin, Collins' head man in the Intelligence unit, asked Dolan one morning if he would "get" him. "I said I would if he gave me Bolster for cover," Dolan told me. "So about nine in the morning we waited in the foyer of the hotel and as he crossed the foyer, I let him have one in the heart and one in the head, and another for good measure, and I walked out."

In the Civil War, Joe Dolan, now a commandant in the Free State Army, shot more men, his fellow countrymen. He was on the back of the armoured car, Slievenamon, when it ran into the ambush at Béal na mBláth on August 22, 1922, and Michael Collins was shot dead.

After the Troubles and when he left the Army, Joe Dolan had a number of jobs, ending up as an attendant in a dispensary. He lived his last years on the borderline of poverty.

To shoot anybody in cold blood must be one of the hardest things for any human being to do, though I've been told by people who did it that it gets easier after the first time. Nevertheless, some of Dolan's comrades in the Tan War ended their days in mental hospitals. and some of them suffered recurring nightmares for many years after "peace" had been established in Ireland.

I asked Joe Dolan about it one night. Did his conscience ever trouble him, I wanted to know. He answered candidly: "About ten years after the Troubles, I was worried, and I went to the Jesuits. I told one of them my problem, and he said that

I had no reason to blame myself: I was a soldier fighting a war and I was acting under orders, just the same as many Irishmen who killed Germans in France and Turks in Gallipoli under orders from the British Army. You must also remember that in 1919–21, the British were shooting and torturing our fellows and burning homes, so that made it easier to shoot them."

When he died, his coffin was draped in the Tricolour and a small band of his former comrades, now old and shrunken, urged their weary bones to some semblance of military order as they fired three volleys over his grave to the sound of the Last Post.

And I wondered. In his young days, Joe Dolan was a terrorist, a thug, a murderer. He was a man of vah'lance who had no mandate from the people. After the war had been won, he was a patriot, a gallant freedom fighter, one of the brave band who helped to found the State. Come to think of it, Archbishop Makarios, Jomo Kenyatta, de Valera and many others made the same transition.

Marino Branch
Brainse Marglann Mhuirine
Tel: 8336297

Chapter 15

Morgue

He was round. That's the only way I can describe him. His body, clad in a navy-blue uniform, was round. His silver-rimmed spectacles were round. His peaked cap, pushed to the back of his head, was round. And his red face was round. Like most small, round, red-faced men, he was cheerful and a chatterbox, though his calling would seem to be more suited to a long, thin, melancholy, pale-faced man, for he was the assistant in the Morgue, or to give it its full title, the Dublin City Coroner's Court.

It was a freezing day some years ago; sleet and rain and slush and everything came pouring down from the heavens as I went into the morgue. Cheerful, he greeted me.

"That's a bad day sir, reminds me of the winter of '47. Now, there was a winter for you, right for three months after Christmas, I thought it'd never thaw. Ah, that was a busy time for us. You know, we're always busy here. Accident cases? Ah, they're the worst. Some of them mangled so bad their own mothers don't know them. I've seen mothers, aye, and fathers too, vomiting on the floor looking at the remains of their own children. It's all these cars on the road and all that drink."

He had to pause for breath and I asked him what time the

body could be removed. Lighting a cigarette, for I needed one, I shoved the packet towards him.

"Never touch them sir. Oh not me. You want to see the lungs like I do – all dirty-brown and shrivelled and hard. Oh, no, I gave them up years ago after the coroner – a lovely man – showed me the first lungs I ever saw. That was forty years ago. I'm seventy now and never had a cough in my life."

Someone else had entered the gloomy room, and he switched his attention: "That the habit for Mrs Browne? Ah yes, just bring it in there and leave it. I'll fix it up after. No hurry. Yes, it is a filthy day. Good luck to you now, see you tomorrow."

"Now, sir," he turned to me, "you were saying? Ah, yes, well d'ye know, that was a lovely woman. Five feet eight. That's right. Measured her for the coffin myself. You'd never think there was anything wrong with her. Fine healthy young woman. All the organs in perfect condition. Ah, yes, still, you never know, do you? Here today and gone tomorrow. The lungs now, perfect. Had them in these hands myself. The liver, all right too. Stomach nothing wrong. You'd wonder what makes them do it, wouldn't you? Sometimes it'd be young ones pregnant, maybe young ones from the country and they're ashamed to let their people know. But sure that couldn't be the case with her, sure it couldn't? Wasn't she a married lady? You'll always know with the gas. Turns the blood a sort of pink, y'know.

"But the drugs now, they're different. The boss, a gentleman if there ever was one, tells me everything. I'm sure I could do a p.m. myself, with all the years I'm watching him and helping him. I have to prepare the corpses for him, you know, wash them, tidy them up and sometimes make the first cuts. It's always the heart and the lungs and the stomach first.

"What was I saying? Ah, yes, about the drugs. There's an awful lot of them brought in here from the drugs now. I don't know what's coming over the world at all. Last week I had a young one, lovely young girl, not married, from the country. An overdose. The mother and father were heartbroken. Well-to-do, too, father a big job here in Dublin. The young one was going to university, must have got in with a wrong set. That's what happens to them all now, think they're big, and they'll never get into the habit – ha ha, didn't mean that sir, sure we'll all be in the habit one day, ha ha.

"But what was I saying? Ah yes, this beautiful kid: money, education, everything. And an overdose. Beautiful corpse she was. Ah my God, you should have seen her . . . only twenty-two as well.

"Last week too, we had a young woman picked out of the canal. Young married woman, not much more than a girl. Threw herself in. Pregnant she was too. They said the oul' mind had gone. Mind you, the boss here is very good. Doesn't like to give a verdict of suicide if he can avoid it. You know the way people'd talk – the neighbours'd say the whole family was a bit, well, not right, you know. So it's always the balance of the mind that was disturbed, you know. That way, they can get a Christian burial. Though to my own mind, it doesn't matter a bit where they put you when you're gone. Sure you won't know or care, eh, ha ha. As we used to say, 'if they don't bury you for show, they'll bury you for stink,' ha ha.

"But I'm sorry, sir. You were asking me what time the body will be released? Well, now, I shouldn't rightly tell you this, because there was to be an inquest like, but you can take it out about five this evening, I'll fix it. You can get the hearse here about five, and I'll make sure it's alright. The p.m. is done, and the inquest can be held later. We don't like to drag out the agony for the relations, you know. Would you like to see her, private like? No trouble at all. No? Well, alright sir. You're going? Right. Be back at five, and I'll open the side gate for the hearse, myself, and I'll hold up the traffic to let you out. Always do that. Sure we're all the one when all's said and done, aren't we?

"Oh, by the way, sir, you're not the husband, are you? Ah, that's good. Well, she was a lovely woman. We'll have her looking well for the removal. Bye now, sir. See you at five."

Fortunately there was a pub at the corner.

Chapter 16

Wake

The first wake I ever attended put me off them for many a long year. I was about five years old when Mrs Bowes died. She was, at least to me, an old old woman, small, white-haired and kindly, invariably dressed in black, with pearl buttons on her high-necked blouse, and when she went out in the street she always wore what we called the widow's bonnet, a sort of lacy affair, black, of course, that looked for all the world like a weaving of weeds.

Mrs Bowes lived in the front parlour of the tenement and she was waked in the fashion befitting a lady of some dignity. True, the neighbours sat up with the body the night before the funeral, but there was no hooley, no melodeon, and no booze, though saucers of snuff were placed on the tables around the coffin.

My grandmother, God rest her, who hailed from the county of Galway, had a sense of the fitness of these things. She repaired to the snug of Bill Bushe's pub with some of the other old women for a few gills of porter, and later came up to take me, her favourite grandson, to the parlour to bid farewell to the departed.

Life, and particularly darkness, held untold terrors for me at that time. Darkness doesn't worry me (too much) now. The parlour was dark, lit only by the three candles which framed the head and shoulders of the old woman in the coffin. The neighbours, all old, sat along the four walls of the room, talking in low voices and sniffing snuff. When my grannie walked in with me by the hand, the neighbours broke off their mumbling conversations to "There y'are Mrs Thornton" her, and "How's the little man himself, God bless him" me.

The little-man-himself-God-bless-him was paralysed with fright. It was late and it was dark. And Death was an alien and frightening thing, for Sister Dorothy in Gardiner Street Infants' School had left us in no doubt that hell was a terribly real place, and damn few escaped it. The little-man-himself-God-bless-him tried unsuccessfully to free his hand from his grannie's and run, even up the dark stairs to the light of his own place.

But Grannie, apart altogether from her few gills of porter, believed that wakes and funerals should be carried out properly, and after she had landed a rather portery kiss on the still face of her dead crony in the coffin, lifted me bodily and forced my childish face to nuzzle the cold, shrunken visage of the corpse.

That night, and for many nights afterwards, I had screaming nightmares, and for many a long year, I never visited a hospital nor attended a funeral until I knew the corpse had been safely coffined.

It was many years later that I attended another wake, so vastly different from my first that only for the fact I was older and wiser, I might have thought it was a celebration, for there was laughter and song and jokes and music and oceans of beer and spirits and while it, too, carried on long into the night, every light in the place was ablaze.

It was the wake of the Theatre Royal on the night the fire curtain with all its enduring advertisements – the Happy Ring House, Yardley Lavender and the rest – had come down on the stage for the last time. The death of the Royal was decreed by the moguls of the J. A. Rank organisation, and the late Louis Elliman, the boss of the Royal, issued the command: "Let there be a fitting wake; let the staff and the artists drink the bars dry."

The band was there: Mickey Reynolds, the trumpeter, and Jimmy Bayle, the gobstick player, and all the rest. The Royalettes were there: Eileen O'Connor and the other girls, and of course, Alice and Babs, who had made the Royalettes into one of the greatest dancing troupes possibly in the world. The stage-hands, the flymen Dick Doyle, Billy Dunne, and Peter Glennon, one of the best feathers ever to win an Irish title, were there. The usherettes, Margaret and Snowy and Florrie were there, the ushers, Paddy Judge, Paddy Woodbyrne, Peter Kearns, the projectionists, the electricians, the boilermen, the cleaners, the barmaids and the artistes who had walked the boards during the Emergency, the first one, I mean. Jack Cruise, Noel Purcell, Pauline Forbes, Jimmy O'Dea, Peggy Dell, Sean Mooney, Danny Cummins and many others put in an appearance to say goodbye.

I was there, not because I had worked in the Royal, nor had I ever performed there, but because I was invited, and in any case, the Kellys had a vested interest in the place. Oul' Billy, God be good to him, was stage manager, Chris my brother was assistant stage manager, Margaret and Nellie had been usherettes, and Maurice had been a projectionist in the Regal. And I had been in the Royal regularly from the time I was six; the staff got a weekly pass, and my mother, may she rest in peace, often brought a few of us there, to keep us quiet for a few hours.

Mr Elliman, possibly because he thought I was part of the furniture, was always friendly with me, and though to the staff he was always "Mr Louis", between him and me it was "Bill" and "Louis".

The Theatre Royal is no more. Instead it is a profitable office block, known as Hawkins House. It was more than just a theatre; it was an institution in Irish life, for not only the native Dubliners frequented it, but every visitor from the provinces went there.

I can remember, many years ago, the Celebrity Concerts on Saturdays when the world's greatest artistes appeared on the stage of the Hawkins Street theatre. I remember Albert Sandler, the violinist, Fritz Kreisler, the violinist, who appeared in a red shiny dressing gown, and Eileen Joyce, of the D'Oyly Carte company.

I was backstage when they were fitting up the screen for the talkies, for the new cine-variety programmes designed to catch the slightly flagging crowds, and was astounded at the two big horns, just like old-fashioned gramophone horns, which were placed behind the screen to provide the sound.

The Royal had a circus with elephants and lions, and they were none too popular with the stage hands who had to break up the ring, move the cages and clean up after the elephants and horses! The Royal was, I think, the first to have an ice show in Ireland, for which a freezing plant was set up on stage.

In the days of the big bands, Henry Hall, Roy Fox, and Joe Loss packed them in, as did Larry Adler, a slim boyish figure in grey polo neck pullover and grey slacks when he appeared, billed as a "virtuoso of the harmonica". Before him, Borra Minevich and his Harmonica Rascals had shown that the mouth organ could be a serious musical instrument.

Way back in the twenties and thirties, Nervo and Knox,

Lucan and McShane, the Crazy Gang, Flanagan and Allen, G. H. Elliott, Wee Georgie Wood, Gracie Fields, George Formby, and Harry Lauder, entertained the thousands of Dubliners, aye, and the country folk too, when they came to town.

May Devitt and Josef Locke, and the Irish Thrush, Jack Doyle and Movita, held the audience enthralled, and provided much more off-the-cuff entertainment for the backstage staff during their clashes of artistic temperament as soon as the curtain came down.

When oul' Billy was an usher in the Royal, the front house staff always prepared for battle with the students of Trinity and UCD on the night of the annual rag day. Believe it or not, the fire hoses were used many times to repel the rampaging but good-natured students as they tried to gate-crash.

Tom Mix, familiar to earlier generations on the films, came in person to the Royal and, as he paraded on his horse up through O'Connell Street, the crowds, much in the manner of today's teenagers, tore pieces off his horse's tail for souvenirs. But Gene Autry, the singing cowboy, really set the country alight, and caused the Irish skies to be rent, day and night, with "Ay Ay Ay Ays", after his stint on the Hawkins Street stage, just before World War II broke out in 1939. I well remember a dozen of us cycling in from Portmarnock to see Gene and hear his signature tune, "South of the Border".

Cine-variety, as they called it, meant you got a three-hour show, with live entertainment and film, for as little as a shilling. And the old, the cold and the unemployed hastened to Hawkins Street to spend the best part of the afternoon and evening in the warm and lovely world of make-believe in the theatre. A common belief was that many of them brought their lunches, for you weren't put out at the end of the performance.

That delightful euphemism, the Emergency, recently resurrected as a "device" according to a Minister of State, threw the theatre in Ireland back on its own resources, and the Royal for five years and more proved once again that this country could be self-sufficient. Mr Louis produced the shows as "T. R. Royle", and the public lapped them up. Jimmy O'Dea and Maureen Potter trod the boards there; Dickie Forbes proved his talent as a scriptwriter. Alice and Babs devised world standard dance routines for the Royalettes, and Jimmy Campbell staged musical vignettes of the highest quality. The stage staff and props excelled themselves in staging playlets to the music of Tchaikovsky's *1812 Overture,* the *William Tell Overture*, *Fingal's Cave* and other classics played by the orchestra and danced to by the girls.

Noel Purcell and Eddie Byrne in the *Nedser and Nuala* series, Harry Bailey, Jack Cruise, Joe Lynch, Sean Mooney and hundreds of other well-known artistes including Danny Cummins, Hal Roche, Edmund Browne, Joe McNally, and even Eamonn Andrews, climbed to fame via Hawkins Street. One never-to-be-forgotten show in the war years was the Irish Army recruiting spectacular, *The Roll of the Drum*, a theatrical tattoo, which enthralled the 4,000 patrons every day for weeks. The "Roll of the Drum" concluded with the Army Band on stage for the great finale, and the conductor descending a flight of steps from the wings each night to front the band. That is, each night until the fatal one, on which, aided perhaps by Lethe's draughts, he overbalanced, kepi, ceremonial cloak, dress uniform and all, and came head over heels down the steps.

After the Emergency, the world's greatest still came to Mr. Louis. Danny Kaye, sitting at the footlights, holding the audience spellbound for over forty minutes merely by chatting; the tragic and so charismatic Judy Garland, the completely professional Bob Hope, whose show was taped in the wings by a certain local comedian for adaptation at a future date – they kept up the standard.

Katherine Dunham's troupe of dancers, the West Indians, was the most exciting modern ballet seen here. Word of mouth had it that the brazen hussies had appeared topless in sinful London, and there was always the chance that they might forget their bras in Dublin, but they didn't.

Later, the pop idols came, and oul' Billy risked his job to bring down the curtain on Billy Fury. Fury was making obscene gestures with the mike and Billy Kelly didn't approve. He warned the perfomer that that kind of stuff didn't go down in Dublin, and that if he didn't cut it out, the act would be chopped. Fury didn't, and the big red curtain blotted him out from the audience. Louis Elliman congratulated oul' Billy on his stand.

The Royal was a playhouse for over a hundred years. And in that time it became, not merely a playhouse, not merely an entertainment centre, but an institution in Irish life. Few people in the whole of Ireland hadn't been in it at some time or another, at least on the night prior to the all–Ireland final. I thought of all these things at the wake in the rehearsal hall. I thought of the stars I had seen, of the stories told about the old Royal, of the persistent one that worried the night-watchman on his rounds, alone in the dark in the dead of night, that the ghost of Tom Egerton, the manager who had been burned to death in the old, old Royal in 1880, still walked at the witching hour trying to put out the fire. I thought of the ghosts who would always walk around Hawkins Street, perhaps paying a visit to the other Green Room, Mulligans in Poolbeg Street, and I moved away from the group of Royalettes and comedians.

At the end of one of the makeshift counters, I sipped a solo drink poured by Alice the barmaid. Louis Elliman came and stood beside me, and I swear the tears glistened in his eyes.

"Well, Bill?" he said.

"It's a bloody shame, Louis," said I, "all this – all these people – all going. Why? Why? Was it losing that much?"

"The terrible thing," said Louis, "is that the Royal wasn't losing. Not losing money. Just that the masters decided they'd be making more out of an office block. It didn't have to happen."

We saluted each other with silent glasses. Louis Elliman, heartbroken, circulated, smiling and nodding at his people. I set out determinedly to get drunk.

Glossary

CHAPTER 1

Dustcoat	A type of cotton showerproof coat.
Tan War	The War of Independence 1919–21, so called because it involved the Black and Tans, a British Auxiliary undisciplined force.
Oul' dacancy	Old decency (Dublin pronunciation).
Colzoil	Colza oil.
Oul' wans	Dublinese for old ones, old women.
Ruggy	A fight, a row.
Master McGrath	A famous racing greyhound.
Gur cake	A sort of bread–pudding cake, thick and heavy. "Out on gur" meant to have left home or been put out of home without any means of support.
Polis	Dublin pronunciation for police.
Moaning coach	Mourning coach, for close relatives.
The Brian Boru	Public house of that name in the district of Glasnevin.
Trí coiscéim na marbh	Irish for "three steps of the dead", an ancient custom which dictated that anyone out walking who met a funeral had to turn and walk three steps with the cortege, to show that everyone goes the same way home in the long run.
Hooley	Same as céilí in the Irish language, a house party.
Marge	Margarine. Using marge was a sure sign that you couldn't afford butter, and it was a grave offence to let the neighbours know you used marge.
Rale	Real.
Peelers	Policemen.
D.M.P	Dublin Metropolitan Police.

Thruppence	Three pence in old money.
Monto	Infamous brothel area.
Plás Mhuire	St Mary's Place, the name of a school run by the Irish Christian Brothers.
Má tá Gaeilge agat labhair í	"If you know the Irish language, speak it."
The electric	Electricity supply.

CHAPTER 2

Oh, Mother Eye	The opening lines of a hymn, "Oh, Mother, I could weep for mirth." There was a pause for breath between the "I" and "could".
Maggie Ryan	Slang name for margarine.
Six Mass	Mass at 6 a.m.
Twenty-five bob	Twenty-five shillings (old money).
Half-a-crown	Two shillings and sixpence.

CHAPTER 3

Baden Powell Scouts	The original Boy Scout movement. Only non-Catholics joined them. "Our" lot was the CBSI, the Catholic Boy Scouts of Ireland.
Kevin Barry	An 18-year old student hanged by the British during the War for Independence as an active IRA member, following an ambush in which British soldiers were killed.

CHAPTER 4

Banshee	Irish for fairy woman. The superstition still is that the Banshee follows certain Irish families and keens a warning of an impending death.
Féar Gorta	Irish for hungry grass. Patches of bewitched earth around the country; anyone stepping on this would become weak and starve to death, if he didn't get off it pretty quickly.

Jack O' Lantern	Will-o'-the-wisp.
Dead House	The mortuary was always called the Dead House in Dublin.

CHAPTER 5

Loaf	English slang. A loaf of bread is a head.

CHAPTER 7

McBirney's	A big store, a landmark in Dublin, now closed.
Jackie Carey	Irish international footballer.
Fíon na Filíochta	Irish for "the wine of poetry".
Ag Críost an Síol	Irish for "Christ has the seed".
Do Cuirfinn-se Féin mo Leanbh a Codladh	"I'd put my child to sleep."
Crónán na mBeach	"The droning of the bees."
Oisín	Legendary son of the legendary hero Fionn Mac Cumhaill
Paddy McGrath	Son of Joe McGrath, founder of the Irish Hospital Sweepstakes.
Taoiseach	Title, meaning "chief" in Irish, adopted under Minister, who was at the time Éamon de Valera.

CHAPTER 8

D.T.P.S.	Dublin Typographical Provident Society, the printers' trade union at that time.
Dakota	A printing works, near the markets area in Dublin.
Lino	A typesetting machine.
An Tóstal	A series of festivals held in the fifties.
Catacombs	Basements in Fitzwilliam Square area in various Bohemian writers and artists lived.

BILL KELLY

Big Bill	The nom de plume under which I wrote the *Sunday Press* column.
Brase and Sauerschweig	A German and a Swiss, musicians who were brought in to command the Irish Army School of Music set up after the British left three parts of Ireland, following the War of Independence.
GAA	Gaelic Athletic Association, formed to revive Irish nationalism, particularly in the realm of sport.
The Tower	The nearest public house.
Mount Jerome	A cemetery opposite Harolds Cross Park.
Oliver	The Sports Editor of the *Irish Press* at the time.
Nick Rackard	A famous hurler and Gaelic footballer who was an alcoholic.

CHAPTER 9

Sally Ann	Slang term for the Salvation Army.
UDC, TC, etc.	Various local authorities.
Minor	Archaic sporting cliché for one point, in hurling and Gaelic football.

CHAPTER 10

Kippure	A peak in the Wicklow Mountains on which Radio Telefis Éireann has mounted a transmitter and mast.
Nutters	Madmen.
Paddy	A much favoured brand of Irish whiskey.

CHAPTER 11

The Stadium	The National Stadium, headquarters of amateur boxing in Ireland.
Widda Maher's	A pub, a well-known landmark for sports followers.
J. Arthur organisation.	J. Arthur Rank, head of the Rank film

A boyo	A wild, feckless, amoral young man.
Bórd na gCon	The Greyhound Board, set up by the government to control and organise greyhound track racing and coursing. Also suspected of being a good outlet for jobs for loyal party supporters, like all semi-state and state bodies in Ireland some time ago.
Grádh	Irish for love.
The Curragh	Race track in Kildare, the headquarters of Irish racing.
Red Bank	A well-known restaurant which eventually failed and is now a Roman Catholic Church.

CHAPTER 12

Soldiers of the Rearguard	Anti-Treaty soldiers in the Civil War.
Belvedere	Expensive private school conducted by the Jesuits. Dubliners say "if you went to Belvedere, you'd always have a job".
Document No. 2	De Valera's alternative to the draft Treaty which ended the War of Independence. Not even top lawyers could distinguish a difference of any consequence between the two documents.
Stair Seanchas na hÉireann Cuid II	Condensed History of Ireland Part 2 in Cló Gaedhalach, Irish type face.
I 1916 bhí Éirigh Amach	"In 1916 there was a Rising."
Henry Street	The street in which Radio Éireann, the state radio station was situated, in the General Post Office building.

CHAPTER 13

Mise Éire	"I am Ireland", title of a poem by Patrick Pearse, one of the executed leaders of the Easter Rising in 1916.

A stór	"My precious."
The heart of the rowl	The heart of the roll, a grand type of person.
Shadda	Dublin pronunciation of shadow.
Slán agat	Irish for goodbye, literally "Health be with you".
Cutline	Mealbreak.
Moocher	One who never had money and scrounged drink.
Oul' china	Close friend.

CHAPTER 14

Vah'lence	Upperclass English person's pronunciation of "violence", aped by a lot of Irish politicians.
Béal na mBláth	Irish place name, officially Béal Átha na Bláiche, meaning "mouth of the ford of the buttermilk".

CHAPTER 16

Oul' Billy	My father, the last stage manager of the Theatre Royal. "Oul" to distinguish between him and me.

Poolbeg wishes to
thank you

for buying a Poolbeg book.

If you enjoyed this why not
visit our website:

www.poolbeg.com

and get another book delivered
straight to your home or to
a friend's home!

All books despatched within 24 hours.

POOLBEG

WHY NOT JOIN OUR MAILING LIST
@ www.poolbeg.com and get some
fantastic offers on Poolbeg books